Copyright © 2022

Publishing house : Independently published

1st Edition

ISBN: 9798882769832

Author
Michele Donnelly
micheledonnelly@gmail.com

Index

Introduction

Welcome to *Creative Writing: Tools and Techniques for Discovering Your Narrative Potential* . Are you ready to immerse yourself in the wonderful world of creative writing, where words come to life and imaginary worlds materialize on the page? If you've ever dreamed of writing a story that captures the reader's imagination or exploring fantasy worlds through words, you're in the right place. This book is designed to guide you on the wonderful journey of creative writing, giving you the tools and knowledge you need to turn your ideas into engaging and memorable stories.

Creative writing is a fascinating and fulfilling journey that can take you to places you never imagined and bring out stories that reside deep within your soul. In these pages, we'll not only explore the fundamentals of fiction writing and writing techniques, but we'll also guide you through a series of thought-provoking exercises designed to unleash your creativity and inspire your imagination; creative writing is not only an art, but also a discipline that can be refined and developed with constant practice and the application of specific techniques. Throughout these pages, we'll explore the fundamentals of narrative, different writing styles, the process of character development, and much more. Through practical exercises, both throughout the various chapters and in an *ad hoc chapter* , we will guide you in unleashing your creativity and cultivating your unique voice as a writer.

Whether you are an aspiring writer eager to begin your literary journey or a seasoned author looking for new perspectives, "Scrittura Viva" is here for you. Prepare to experience the joy of creation and discover the pleasure of transforming your ideas into vibrant, engaging stories. We are excited to accompany you on this adventure and see the wonderful stories that will emerge from your pen. Welcome to your new home of creativity.

Chapter one

Fundamentals of Creative Writing

"Writing is easy. All you have to do is sit at a typewriter and bleed."

ERNEST HEMINGWAY

Definition of Creative Writing

Creative writing is the art of expressing ideas, emotions and stories through words. It is a process that goes beyond simple communication and involves imagination, curiosity and passion. Creative writers play with words, creating unique worlds, characters, and situations.

Creative writing can manifest itself in various ways, such as fiction, poetry, articles, play scripts, and much more. It is fertile ground for linguistic exploration, experimentation and innovation and spans a wide range of genres and styles, from fantasy tales to historical fiction, from poetry to creative non-fiction. What all these forms have in common is their ability to convey emotions, stimulate the imagination and connect with audiences in a deep and meaningful way.

Creative writers aren't limited to grammatical rules or conventions. They are free to break barriers and invent new forms of expression. Creative writing is a personal journey, a way to give voice to our visions and passions, to express ourselves, explore our passions and give voice to our ideas. It is a process of personal discovery and self-expression that can lead to greater awareness of ourselves and the world around us.

In short, creative writing is an art that connects us with our inner world and with others. It is a gift that we can cultivate and share with the world.

Fundamental Elements of Narrative

Storytelling is an ancient art that has its roots in stories passed down orally through generations. Every story, regardless of genre or form, is built on a set of fundamental elements that give it structure and meaning.

1. **Characters** : Characters are the main actors of the story, those who carry the action forward and with whom the reader can identify. From the simple country girl to the brave knight, characters are the beating heart of the narrative, and their development and characterization are essential to an engaging and memorable story.

2. **Plot** : The plot is the underlying theme of the story, the series of events that follow one another and that lead the characters through a series of challenges, conflicts and transformations. A good plot is full of suspense, twists and moments of climax that keep the reader glued to the pages.

3. **Setting** : The setting provides the context in which the events of the story take place. It can be a fantasy world populated by magical creatures or a modern and chaotic city. The setting is not just a decorative backdrop, but can profoundly influence the tone and meaning of the story.

4. **Theme** : The theme is the main message or idea that the story tries to communicate. It can be about love, forgiveness, courage, justice or any other universal theme. A well-developed theme provides the story with depth and meaning, giving the reader something to think about even after they close the book.

It is through the combination of these elements that a rich and complex narrative takes shape, capable of capturing the reader's attention and transporting him on an exciting journey. Throughout this book, we will explore how to use these elements effectively and creatively to create works that capture audiences' imaginations and transport them to worlds of fantasy and adventure.

Creating Vivid and Engaging Characters

Characters are the beating heart of any story. They are the ones who move the narrative forward, who face challenges, who grow and change over the course of the story. Creating vivid, compelling characters is key to engaging the reader and making the story memorable. A well-developed character is like a real person, with motivations, challenges, and emotions that make him or her unique and interesting to the reader. To achieve this goal, it is important to consider three main dimensions: physical, psychological and social.

These will be listed below accompanied by examples of famous people.

Physical Dimension

This dimension includes the external aspects of the character, such as physical appearance, age, gender, race and clothing. However, the physical dimension goes beyond the superficial appearance and also includes body language, gestures and facial expressions that help define the character's personality.

1. **Harry Potter** - "Harry Potter" series by JK Rowling:

   - Physical Description: Messy black hair, almond-shaped green eyes, lightning bolt-shaped scar on forehead.

   - Distinctive Physical Appearance: Round black-rimmed glasses, thickly curled white shirt, faded sneakers.

   - Physical Details That Reflect Personality: Sloppy clothes suggest her modest nature and little interest in fashion; the scar on his forehead is a hallmark of his past and his connection to Voldemort, highlighting his importance in the wizarding world; his round glasses and lightning bolt scar reflect his uniqueness and his destiny as

The Chosen One, symbols of his courage and determination in facing adversity.

2. **Hermione Granger** - JK Rowling's "Harry Potter" series:

   - Physical Description: Curly brown hair, slightly prominent front teeth, thick glasses.

   - Distinctive physical appearance: Simple and practical clothing, often with a book in hand.

   - Physical details that reflect personality: Her confident posture and the way she carries herself suggest determination and self-confidence.

3. **Katniss Everdeen** - Series "Hunger Games" by Suzanne Collins:

   - Physical Description: Dark hair and gray eyes, slim and agile.

   - Distinctive Physical Appearance: Her bow and arrows, symbolizing her role as a hunter and her ability to survive.

   - Physical details that reflect personality: His often serious and resolute expression suggests a steely determination and a sense of responsibility towards his family and other tributes.

Psychological dimension

This dimension concerns the internal aspects of the character, such as his emotions, his thoughts, his beliefs and his motivations. A well-developed character has a complex and authentic psychology, which reflects his history, his experiences and his relationships with other characters.

1. **Harry Potter** - "Harry Potter" series by JK Rowling:

    - Emotions and Thoughts: Harry feels a deep sense of loss and loneliness due to the death of his parents and the hostile environment in which he grew up; longs for a sense of belonging and family, despite the difficulties he encounters in relationships with his relatives; anger and frustration towards those who have hurt his parents and friends push him to act against injustice.

    - Beliefs: He firmly believes in the importance of friendship and love, which guide him in his actions and relationships; has a strong belief in fighting the forces of evil and injustice, demonstrating faith in the power of honesty and courage; His family values , such as honesty and courage, are central to his decisions and behavior.

2. **Holden Caulfield** - "Young Holden" by JD Salinger:

    - Emotions and thoughts: Deeply dissatisfied with the adult world, with a strong sense of alienation and disillusionment.

- Beliefs: Critical of society's hypocrisy and superficiality, eager for authenticity and sincerity.

- Motivations: Searching for a sense of belonging and meaning in his life, often confused and struggling with himself.

3. **Lisbeth Salander** - "Millennium" series by Stieg Larsson:

- Emotions and thoughts: Marked by a traumatic past, with deep anger and a desire for justice.

- Beliefs: Distrust of authorities and the system, with a strong sense of personal justice.

- Motivations: The search for revenge against those who have harmed her and the desire to protect those she loves.

Social dimension

This dimension concerns the character's relationships and interactions with others in the context of the story. This includes family, friends, enemies, and the community in which he lives. A character's social relationships influence his actions and decisions, adding complexity to his characterization.

1. **Harry Potter** - "Harry Potter" series by JK Rowling:

- Family Relationships: Harry grows up in a hostile environment with his aunt and uncle, the Dursleys, after the death of his parents. However, the memory of his deceased parents inspires and guides him throughout his life.

- Community Interactions: Harry has significant interactions with a variety of people in the wizarding community, including classmates, teachers, and members of the Order of the Phoenix; his friendship with Ron and Hermione is a cornerstone in his life, and his special relationship with the headmaster of Hogwarts, Albus Dumbledore, helps him grow as a person and a wizard.

- Role in Society: Harry takes a central role in magical society due to his connection to Voldemort and his role as The Chosen One; he is considered a figure of hope and inspiration to many wizards and witches, and his determination to fight evil makes him a respected figure within the magical community.

- Start of form

2. **Atticus Finch** - "To Kill a Mockingbird" by Harper Lee:

- Family Relationships: A loving and caring father to his children, Scout and Jem, who tries to teach them respect and empathy.

- Community Interactions: Respected and valued by Maycomb residents for his integrity and courage in addressing racism and injustice.

- Role in Society: A lawyer committed to defending justice and civil rights, even when it is unpopular to do so.

3. **Lena Haloway** - "Delirium" by Lauren Oliver:

   - Family Relationships: Raised in a family devoted to emotional control and romantic relationships, but with a complicated relationship with her mother and sister.

   - Community Interactions: Initially conformist and obedient to the rules of her dystopian world, but later rebellious and determined to follow her heart.

   - Role in Society: A girl who challenges the oppressive norms of the society she lives in and seeks the freedom to love whoever she wants.

Creating three-dimensional characters requires attention to detail and depth of characterization. By integrating these three dimensions, writers can bring to life characters who feel real, who face challenges, grow and evolve throughout the story, capturing the attention and hearts of readers.

Narrative Structure: Introduction, Development, Climax, Conclusion

Narrative structure is the backbone of any engaging story. It provides a framework on which to build the narrative and guide the reader through an exciting and fulfilling journey. In this chapter, we will explore the four key elements of narrative structure: the introduction, development, climax, and conclusion. We'll see how these elements work together to create tension, stir emotion, and bring the story to a satisfying conclusion.

Introduction

The introduction is the foundation on which the entire narrative structure is built. It is the moment in which readers cross the threshold of the world created by the author, immersing themselves in the details of the setting and getting to know the protagonists. This initial phase is crucial as it establishes the foundation for what will follow, creating expectations and generating interest in the reader.

During the introduction, authors must captivate the reader's attention by skillfully providing enough information to arouse curiosity without smothering the narrative with superfluous details. It is important to find a balance between the presentation of the characters and the description of the setting, allowing the reader to gradually immerse themselves in the world of the story.

In this phase the foundations are laid for the main "conflict" of the story. While the conflict may not be explicitly outlined from the start, the introduction offers clues and hints that set the stage for future events. This can be through suspended dialogue, ambiguous descriptions, or enigmatic events that capture the reader's interest and encourage them to keep reading to find out what happens next.

Finally, the introduction should establish the tone and atmosphere of the story, which can range from an atmosphere of suspense and mystery to one of calm and serenity, depending on the author's genre and style. This first glimpse of the story should be captivating enough to intrigue the reader and invite them to fully immerse themselves in the narrative, preparing them for the gripping events that come next.

Development

Development is the central phase of storytelling, where the story comes to life through a series of events, conflicts and transformations. During this phase, the characters face a series of increasingly demanding challenges that push them beyond their limits and lead them to grow and change throughout the story.

One of the main functions of development is to delve deeper into the story's main conflict and evolve characters in response to the challenges they face. This can include internal conflicts, where characters must contend with their own fears, doubts and weaknesses, as well as external conflicts with other characters or antagonistic forces.

During development, authors have the opportunity to explore complex themes and bring out the characters' deeper motives. This phase can include moments of personal growth, introspection and change, which lead the characters to a greater awareness of themselves and the world around them.

Additionally, development provides the opportunity to expand the story's setting and introduce new characters and subplots that enrich the main plot. These additional elements can add depth and complexity to the story, creating a richer and more engaging world for the reader to explore.

Finally, development is where narrative tension builds, gradually leading to the creation of a compelling climax. Authors must skillfully manage the pace of the narrative, keeping the reader engaged and eager to know what will happen next, until the climax of the story.

Climax

The climax is the culmination of narrative tension within a story, the moment of maximum intensity in which the main conflict reaches its peak and the destinies of the characters hang in the balance. It is the crucial turning point that determines the course of events and the final outcome of the story.

During the climax, the characters' actions reach their most critical and decisive point. Decisions made at this time have significant consequences and can radically change the course of the plot. It is the moment when the conflicts that have been built up throughout the development of the story are finally addressed and resolved, often through epic scenes, moments of great tension and shocking revelations.

The climax is also the time when the characters show their true character and their true motivations come to light. It's here that we see how far the protagonists are willing to go to achieve their goals, and where their limits are tested. This phase can also include moments of redemption or ruin for characters, where their past actions have unavoidable consequences in the present.

Finally, the climax is the moment when narrative tension reaches its peak, keeping readers or viewers glued to the page or screen. It is a moment of great emotion and suspense, where the audience is fully involved in the story and eager to discover its outcome. Mastery in building the climax is essential to the success of any story, as this is where the story reaches its climax and leaves a lasting impression on the audience.

In cinema, the climax is often characterized by epic scenes, big turning points and crucial revelations that keep the viewer glued to the screen. Here are some famous examples of climaxes in films **[SPOILER WARNING]** :

The Lord of the Rings: The Return of the King: In the climax of this fantasy epic, the battle of Middle-earth reaches its climax as the forces of good and evil clash in the final battle for the fate of Middle-earth.

Star Wars: Episode V - The Empire Strikes Back: In the climax of this film, Luke Skywalker faces Darth Vader in an epic lightsaber duel, culminating in the shocking revelation of his father's true identity.

The Godfather - Part II: In the climax of this cinematic classic, Michael Corleone faces the consequences of his actions as he seeks to consolidate his criminal power and protect his family from internal and external threats.

The Matrix: In the climax of this groundbreaking science fiction film, Neo faces Agent Smith in a spectacular fight for the fate of humanity within the Matrix.

Titanic: In the climax of this epic story of love and tragedy, the Titanic hits an iceberg and sinks in the Atlantic Ocean, endangering the lives of the protagonists and passengers on board .

Conclusion

The conclusion represents the moment when all the plot threads are finally pulled together and the main conflict finds a resolution. It is the point at which readers or viewers see the final consequences of the characters' actions and discover the final fate of the story. This phase is crucial to making sense of the narrative and providing a satisfying closure for the audience.

During the conclusion, the authors have the opportunity to answer all the questions raised during the development of the story and to highlight the deeper meaning of the narrative. This can include moments of revelation, where well-kept secrets are finally revealed, and moments of epiphany , where characters gain a new understanding of themselves and the world around them.

Additionally, the conclusion provides an opportunity to show the characters' change and growth throughout the story. Authors can demonstrate how the protagonists learned from their experiences and faced challenges to become better people. This can include moments of redemption for characters who have made mistakes throughout the story, as well as moments of triumph for those who have struggled to achieve their goals.

Ultimately, the conclusion should provide a satisfying closure for the audience, resolving all major conflicts convincingly and leaving a feeling of fulfillment and satisfaction. It is a time when readers or viewers can reflect on the story as a whole and draw their own conclusions about its significance and impact. A well-executed conclusion is essential to making sense of the narrative and leaving a lasting impression on the audience.

Chapter two

Writing styles and techniques

> *"Writing is like playing the piano. You can learn techniques, but it's the art behind it that truly makes the music extraordinary."*
>
> *DAVID LEVITHAN*

Writing is a versatile and dynamic art, offering authors a wide range of tools and techniques to express their creativity. In this chapter, we'll dive into the fascinating world of writing styles and techniques, exploring the different ways authors can bring their stories to life and take readers on an unforgettable journey.

Choosing a **narrative style** is one of the first decisions authors face when they begin writing a story. First-person narration offers an immediate and intimate experience, allowing readers to see the world through the eyes of the narrator character. On the other hand, third-person narration offers a broader perspective, allowing authors to explore more characters and settings within the story.

In addition to choosing narrative style, authors must also consider the effective use of description and **setting** . A vivid, detailed description can transport readers to another world, allowing them to fully immerse themselves in the story and its characters. However, it is important to find a balance between detail and conciseness, avoiding weighing down the story with excessive details that can slow down the pace of the narrative.

Dialogue is another key element of writing, offering readers a unique opportunity to learn about characters and their psychology . Realistic and meaningful dialogue can add depth and complexity to the story, allowing characters to develop and interact in an authentic and engaging way.

Ultimately, the **narrative voice** is what brings the story to life, giving it a distinctive and unique character. Authors can experiment with different narrative voices to achieve different effects, tailoring the narrative voice to the tone and genre of the story.

In this chapter, we'll explore each of these elements in detail, offering practical advice and tips on how to effectively use writing styles and techniques to create engaging and memorable stories. Through practical examples and exercises, readers will learn to make the most of their creative potential and transform their ideas into vibrant, compelling narratives.

Exploring Narrative Styles

Choosing a narrative style is one of the most important decisions a writer must make before starting to write a story. Each narrative style offers a unique perspective through which readers enter the story world and interact with characters. In this chapter, we will explore different modes of storytelling and discover how each influences the reading experience.

First-person narrative

First-person narration is a powerful narrative option that offers readers a highly immersive experience. In this style, the narrator is directly involved in the story, and the reader sees the world through his eyes, feels his emotions, and experiences his experiences in real time. This type of narrative creates an immediate bond between the reader and the protagonist, allowing you to develop a deep emotional connection with the main character. A classic example of first-person narrative is Mark Twain's "The Adventures of Huckleberry Finn," where young Huck Finn tells his story of adventures and personal growth as he travels along the Mississippi River.

Third person narration

Third-person narration gives authors a more detached perspective, allowing them to explore more characters and settings within the story. In this style, the narrator is external to the story and is not part of the characters' world, but can see and know their thoughts, emotions, and actions. This allows authors to create a broader and more nuanced vision of the plot, and to provide the reader with a deeper understanding of the characters and their motivations. A famous example of third-person narration is Jane Austen's "Pride and Prejudice", where the omniscient narrator offers a privileged glimpse into the life and relationships of the Bennet family.

Mixed narrative

Some authors choose to experiment with mixed narrative styles, combining elements of first-person and third-person narrative to create unique effects. This may include using first-person narrative sections to focus on certain characters or key moments in the story, alternating with third-person narrative sections to provide a broader view of the plot. This hybrid approach can add depth and complexity to storytelling, allowing authors to explore characters' experiences from different perspectives. An example of mixed narration is "A Song of Ice and Fire" by George RR Martin, where the chapters are narrated by several characters in the first person, offering a multiple view of the events taking place in the world of Westeros.

These are just examples of the many narrative styles available to authors, and each has its own unique characteristics and advantages. Choosing the right narrative style often depends on the tone and genre of the story, as well as the author's personal vision and preferences. Exploring different storytelling styles can be an exciting way to discover new creative possibilities and find the perfect voice to tell your story.

Effective Use of Description and Setting

Description and setting are key elements in creating a vivid and engaging world within a story. In this chapter, we will explore the importance of using these elements effectively to transport readers to an imaginary place and give them a full sensory experience.

The importance of Description

Description plays a vital role in the art of storytelling, as it allows authors to effectively convey the fictional world of the story to readers. An accurate, detailed description not only provides a visual representation of the surrounding environment, but can also evoke emotion, stimulate the imagination, and engage the reader's senses in an immersive, multi-sensory experience.

A good description is not limited to simply listing the visual details of a place or object, but goes further, capturing the essence and unique atmosphere of what is being described. For example, rather than simply saying a forest is "green," an effective description might evoke the sensation of walking under a canopy of rustling branches, smelling the damp earth and the sound of leaves moving in the wind.

Description can also be used to create a sense of setting and historical context, transporting readers to worlds distant in time and space. Through an accurate description of the physical and cultural characteristics of a place, authors can make readers relive bygone eras or transport them to exotic and fantastical places.

Furthermore, description plays an important role in the characterization of characters, allowing authors to paint vivid and convincing portraits of protagonists and supporting characters of the story. By describing physical traits, facial expressions, body language, and personal details, authors can bring characters to life, making them more realistic and memorable for the reader.

In summary, description is a powerful tool in the hands of authors, capable of transforming a flat and lifeless story into a vibrant and engaging world. Through accurate, evocative, multi-sensory description, authors can transport readers into fantastical worlds and experience unforgettable experiences, capturing their imagination and leaving a lasting impression.

Create an engaging atmosphere

The setting is not simply a static backdrop for the story, but rather a dynamic element that can completely transform the reading experience. One of the main functions of the setting is to create an engaging atmosphere that captures the reader's attention and transports him into the world of the narrative.

Through accurate and detailed description of the surrounding environment, authors can establish an atmosphere that fits the tone and theme of the story. For example, a description of a stormy night with thunder and lightning streaking across the sky can create a sense of tension and suspense, while a description of a peaceful flower garden under the golden light of sunset can evoke a feeling of calm and serenity.

Furthermore, the setting can be used to emphasize certain aspects of the plot or to highlight the emotional changes of the characters. For example, a dark and threatening forest can reflect the state of mind of a character who is scared and on the run, while a flowering landscape can symbolize rebirth and hope.

Another way to create an engaging atmosphere is through the use of symbolic and metaphorical elements in the setting. Authors can use objects, colors, or locations to convey deeper meanings and emphasize story themes. For example, the recurring use of the color blue in a setting can symbolize the characters' sadness or loneliness, while a lone lighthouse on a cliff can represent hope in a dark time.

In summary, creating an engaging atmosphere through setting is essential to transporting readers into the world of the story and making them feel like an integral part of the narrative. Through an accurate, evocative and symbolic description of the surrounding environment, authors can establish an atmosphere that captures the reader's imagination and transports him to fantastic and adventurous worlds, creating an unforgettable reading experience.

Use your senses

The effective use of the senses is essential to create an engaging and immersive setting that captures the reader's attention and transports him into the world of the narrative. In addition to sight, authors must also leverage the other senses - hearing, smell, touch and taste - to create a feeling of realism and authenticity that fully engages the reader.

Describing the sounds of your surroundings can add depth and vibrancy to the scene, allowing the reader to imagine being there. The sound of the wind in the trees, the birds singing in the morning or the sound of a flowing river can transport the reader into the heart of the action and make him feel part of the world described.

Similarly, smell can be a powerful means of evoking emotions and sensations. Describing the smells of the environment - the smell of wet earth after the rain, the scent of flowers in spring or the salty taste of sea air - can make the setting even more alive and engaging for the reader, stimulating their imagination and arousing personal sensations and memories.

Touch is another important sense to consider when describing the setting. Describing the feel of warm sand underfoot, the roughness of a rock face, or the softness of a fabric can add an extra level of realism and tactility to the scene, allowing the reader to fully immerse themselves in the experience.

Finally, taste may be a less used sense in storytelling, but it can still add depth and detail to the setting. Describing the flavors of local foods, traditional drinks or exotic spices can further enrich the description of the environment and provide the reader with a complete multi-sensory experience.

In summary, using the senses effectively in describing the setting is essential to creating an engaging and immersive reading experience. Through the accurate and detailed description of the sounds, smells, tactile sensations and tastes of the surrounding environment, authors can transport readers into the heart of the narrative and make them live unforgettable experiences that remain imprinted in their minds for a long time.

Evoke Emotions and Imagination

The ability to evoke emotions and stimulate the reader's imagination is one of the main goals of setting description. The authors try to convey not only what the characters see, but also what they feel and perceive through the world around them. An evocative description can make the reader feel emotionally involved in the story, making him experience the joys, fears, hopes and pains of the characters.

Through the use of images and metaphors, authors can transform a simple landscape into a scene filled with symbolic meaning. For example, a dark, dense forest can symbolize impending dangers and challenges to face, while a field of wildflowers can represent beauty and innocence.

Additionally, description can be used to elicit specific emotions in the reader, such as joy, sadness, fear, or wonder.

Through the use of evocative and detailed words, authors can convey the emotional tone of the scene and make the reader feel fully immersed in the narrative; What's more, describing the setting can stimulate the reader's imagination, allowing them to clearly visualize the story world in their mind. Good description not only provides visual detail, but also creates a sense of space and depth that makes the story world feel real and tangible.

In conclusion, description can be used to create a sense of anticipation and suspense in the reader, making them want to find out what will happen next. Through the use of suggestions and allusions, authors can keep the reader on their toes and keep them turning the pages to find out what will happen at the end.

In summary, the goal of describing the setting is to transport the reader into an imaginary world and make him live unforgettable experiences through emotions and imagination. Through the use of evocative imagery, deep emotion, and gripping suspense, authors can create stories that capture the reader's attention and leave a lasting impression on their mind and heart.

Below are some practical examples of how the setting can provide a vivid and engaging narrative.

Setting: A futuristic city suspended in the clouds

- Description: Neon-lit streets stretch between skyscrapers that reach into the sky, while flying vehicles zoom above ground traffic. Clouds envelop the skyscrapers, creating an ethereal and surreal atmosphere.

- Effect: The futuristic setting transports the reader to a world of advanced technology and infinite possibilities, inspiring a sense of wonder and adventure.

Setting: An enchanted forest inhabited by mystical creatures

- Description: Impressive trees rise towards the sky, while rivers of light filter through the foliage, creating plays of shadows and reflections. Mystical creatures, such as elves and goblins, move among the trees, while the sound of ancient songs resonates in the air.

- Effect: The enchanted setting transports the reader to a world of magic and wonder, arousing a sense of fascination and mystery.

Setting: An endless desert under a relentless sun

- Description: Sand dunes stretch endlessly as the scorching sun burns in the cloudless sky. The wind raises clouds of sand that dance in the air, while the sound of the wind echoes in the desolate air.

- Effect: The desert setting transports the reader to a world of solitude and desolation, eliciting a sense of isolation and survival.

Setting: A provincial town shrouded in fog

- Description: The half-timbered houses overlook winding streets, while the fog shrouds everything in a veil of mystery. The dim lights of the lanterns create plays of light and shadow, while the sound of footsteps echoes through the deserted streets.

- Effect: The foggy setting transports the reader into a world of secrets and intrigue, eliciting a sense of suspense and tension.

These examples illustrate how a detailed description of the setting can transform ideas into vibrant, immersive narratives, capturing the imagination of audiences and transporting them to fantastical and fascinating worlds.

Exercise 1

Imagine a scene where the protagonist is dealing with a significant loss. Describe their surroundings using details that reflect their mood and emotions. For example, if your protagonist is devastated by loss, you might describe the sky as gray and dark, the wind whispering through the trees as a wail, and the sound of rain falling on the ground as tears.

Exercise 2

Imagine a fantastic and surreal place, like an enchanted forest inhabited by magical creatures. Describe the setting using striking, detailed images that capture the reader's imagination. For example, you might describe trees glowing with a mysterious light, luminous creatures dancing among enchanted flowers, and an air filled with magic and mystery.

Realistic and meaningful dialogue

Dialogue is a key part of narrative, as it offers a direct way for characters to interact and convey crucial information to the reader. However, writing convincing dialogue can be challenging, as it must sound natural and realistic, but at the same time be meaningful to the development of the plot and characters. In this chapter we will explore how to create dialogue that is both authentic and relevant to the story.

Study of everyday conversation

To fully understand how people communicate in everyday life and apply it effectively to dialogue writing, it is important to consider several aspects:

- **Direct observation:** Spend time observing the conversations around you. You can do this in various settings, such as coffee shops, parks, public transportation, or even listening to conversations between friends and family. Take note of how people express themselves, their ways of speaking, the pace of conversation and the use of colloquial expressions.

- **Recording and transcription:** If possible, record conversations and later transcribe what you have recorded. This will allow you to capture subtle details, such as pause times, vocal intonations and non-verbal expressions, which can enrich your dialogues.

Variety of contexts: Explore different situations and social contexts. Conversations between friends will be different from those between colleagues or strangers. Each context has its own specific language and interpersonal dynamics, which can be valuable sources of inspiration for your dialogues.

Character Diversity: See how people of different ages, cultural backgrounds , education levels, and personalities express themselves. This will help you create authentic and varied dialogue for your characters, avoiding stereotypes and making interactions more realistic.

Analysis of conversation patterns: Try to identify recurring patterns in conversations, such as turns of speech, questions and answers, arguments, jokes, etc. These templates can give you an idea of how to structure dialogue in your stories.

Experiment: Once you understand the structure and rhythm of real conversations, experiment with applying these elements to your dialogue writing. Play with variations in tone, pace, and sentence length to make dialogue more vivid and engaging.

Careful observation and analysis of everyday conversations can be valuable resources in improving your dialogue writing skills, allowing you to create character interactions that sound authentic and engaging to the reader.

Exercise 3: Transcription and analysis of the conversation

Objective: Improve your ability to observe and understand everyday conversation to enrich the dialogues in your writings.

Exercise steps:

1. **Transcription:** *Choose a daily conversation to observe and transcribe it faithfully. It could be a conversation between friends, family or colleagues, or even a conversation you overheard in a public place like a cafe or park.*

2. **Participant Analysis:** *Identify the participants in the conversation and note their distinguishing characteristics, such as age, gender, education level, cultural background and personality. This will help you better understand the social and individual context of the conversation.*

3. **Observing speech patterns:** *Observe the speech patterns used during conversation, including tone, register, rhythm, and vocabulary. Pay particular attention to specific regional dialects, slangs or jargons used by participants.*

4. **Structure and content analysis:** *Analyze the structure of the conversation, including topics covered, and turn-taking strategies. Also evaluate the content of the conversation and try to identify any recurring themes or points of interest.*

5. **Reflection on the interpersonal dynamic:** *Reflect on the interpersonal dynamic between the participants in the conversation. Observe the power dynamics, social roles, and nonverbal communication strategies used during the conversation.*

6. **Application to Writing:** *Use your observations and analysis to enrich the dialogue in your writing. Try to integrate the speech patterns, conversation structure,*

and interpersonal dynamics you observed in your transcription into creating realistic and compelling dialogue.

7. **Final Reflection:** *Reflect on the experience and note any new ideas or approaches you have gained to improve your ability to write authentic, well-characterized dialogue.*

Purpose and Characterization of the Dialogues

Dialogues are not simply exchanges of words between characters; they must play a significant role in the plot and characterization. Here's how you can develop dialogue that serves a specific purpose and contributes to character characterization:

1. **Plot Advancement:** Every dialogue should push the story forward in some way. This could mean revealing crucial information, introducing a new conflict, or resolving a tense situation. Before writing dialogue, ask yourself, "What do I want to achieve with this conversation? How will it affect the overall plot?"

2. **Character Revelation:** Dialogue provides a valuable opportunity to develop character personalities and relationships. In addition to what is said, pay attention to how it is said. The way a character speaks, the words he chooses, his tone, and his body language can reveal a lot about his psychology, his motivations, and his relationships with others.

3. **Creating Tension and Conflict:** Dialogue can be used to generate tension and conflict between characters. Use differences of opinion, hidden secrets, and differences of purpose to create dialogue filled with suspense and drama. However, make sure that the conflict always aligns with the personality and goals of the characters involved.

4. **Natural exposition:** Avoid making dialogue sound like devices to convey information to the reader. Information should be integrated into the conversation in a natural way, through discussion and exchange of ideas between characters. If possible, try to show more than tell, allowing the reader to infer information through the context and *subtext* of the dialogue.

5. **Consistency and authenticity:** Make sure dialogue is consistent with the characters' personalities and backgrounds . Each character should have their own way of speaking, with expressions and sayings that reflect their character and history. Maintaining consistency in your dialogue will contribute to the credibility and authenticity of your narrative.

6. **Emotional Subtleties:** Use dialogue to explore characters' emotions and thoughts in a subtle and nuanced way. Many times, the most intense emotions are not expressed openly, but shine through the nuances of language and behavior. Try to capture these emotional subtleties in your dialogue to make the characters more complex and realistic.

When writing dialogue, try to balance its narrative purpose with character characterization, creating interactions that are meaningful, engaging, and authentic.

Exercise 4: Comparing dialogues

Objective: Improve the ability to write dialogues that reflect the individual differences of the characters through direct comparison.

Exercise steps:

1. ***Character Selection:*** *Choose two characters with contrasting personalities or points of view within your story.*

2. ***Identifying Goals:*** *For each character, define a specific goal or desire they want to achieve through the conversation. Make sure these goals conflict or conflict with each other.*

3. ***Dialogue writing:*** *Write a dialogue in which the two characters directly discuss the topics of interest. Use dialogue as a means to explore characters' differences in personalities, opinions, and goals.*

4. ***Analysis:*** *After writing the dialogue, analyze it to identify how the differences between the characters are reflected in their language, tones of voice, and communication strategies. Consider how the comparison helped to further characterize the characters and advance the plot.*

5. ***Review and refine:*** *Reread the dialogue and make any necessary changes to improve the coherence of the characters and the flow of the conversation. Make sure the dialogue is believable and convincing, and that it contributes significantly to the development of the story.*

Exercise 5: Dialogues without words

Objective: Develop the ability to communicate emotions, tension and meaning through non-verbal language in dialogues.

Exercise steps:

1. **Character and Situation Selection:** Choose two characters and imagine a situation in which they cannot or do not want to communicate through words. For example, they may be in an emergency situation where silent communication is needed.

2. **Goal Setting:** Identify the goals or emotions the characters need to communicate during the situation, such as fear, urgency, or determination.

3. **Writing the Scene:** Write the scene without the use of verbal dialogue, focusing instead on nonverbal language, such as gestures, facial expressions, postures, and physical movements. Use these elements to communicate your characters' emotions and goals clearly and convincingly.

4. **Analysis:** After writing the scene, analyze how nonverbal language helped convey the meaning and emotion of the situation. Reflect on how this form of communication integrates with verbal dialogue in your story and how it can be used to further enrich character characterization and plot.

5. **Review and refine:** Reread the scene and make any necessary changes to improve the clarity and effectiveness of the nonverbal communication. Make sure that gestures and facial expressions are consistent with the characters' emotions and goals, and that they contribute significantly to the development of the story.

Eliminate banality in dialogues

Writing dialogue that is authentic and relevant can be a challenge, as it is important to avoid it falling into banality. Here are some tips to eliminate banality and make your dialogues more meaningful:

1. **Purpose and Relevance:** Each dialogue should serve a specific purpose in the plot or character development. Avoid conversations that are superfluous or irrelevant to the story. Always ask yourself, "What is the purpose of this conversation? How does it contribute to the overall narrative?"

2. **Challenge expectations:** Try to avoid clichés and predictable situations in your dialogue. Be creative and experiment with unusual plots and situations. Surprise the reader by introducing unexpected changes in dialogue or revealing surprising information.

3. **Character Depth:** Use dialogue to deepen character characterization. Keep your characters from being flat or stereotypical by giving them complex, multifaceted motivations. Make sure each dialogue reveals something new about the characters, contributing to their growth and development.

4. **Emotional Subtleties:** Try to capture emotional nuances in your dialogue. Human emotions are complex and multifaceted, so avoid stereotypes and superficial

reactions. Leverage the subtleties of language and behavior to convey authentic, engaging emotions.

5. **Unique Style:** Each character should have their own style of speaking and interacting with others. Avoid making all your characters sound the same. Experiment with different speech registers, ways of speaking, and conversation patterns to differentiate characters and make them more realistic.

6. **Gradual Reveal:** Use dialogue to gradually reveal important information about the plot or characters. Avoid direct and overly explicit exposition, which can be banal and uninteresting. Instead, take advantage of subtext and nuance in dialogue to convey information in a more subtle and engaging way.

7. **Review and editing:** Once you have completed writing your dialogue, take the time to review it and edit it if necessary. Try to eliminate superfluous or uninteresting parts, focusing the dialogue on the most significant and relevant moments for the story.

Eliminating banality in dialogue takes practice and attention to detail, but it can make the difference between a flat story and an engaging one. Experiment with different techniques and approaches to make your dialogues more vivid, authentic, and meaningful.

Exercise 6: Rewrite a banal dialogue

Objective: Improve the ability to transform a flat and banal dialogue into a more dynamic, engaging and meaningful one.

Exercise steps:

1. **Dialogue Selection:** *Choose dialogue from your work in progress or write a new one that you find to be flat or banal. This could be a dialogue in which the characters exchange simple pleasantries or less relevant information.*

2. **Dialogue Analysis:** *Analyze the dialogue to identify its weaknesses. Look for sentences or lines that lack tension, interest, or relevance to the plot or character characterization.*

3. **Rewriting the dialogue:** *Rewrite the dialogue, trying to make the sentences more vivid, meaningful and engaging. Introduce elements like conflict, emotion, subtext, or hidden meaning to make the dialogue more intriguing and nuanced.*

4. **Critical examination:** *After rewriting the dialogue, evaluate its quality and effectiveness. Ask yourself whether the new dialogue made the scene more interesting, whether it helped develop the characters or plot more meaningfully, and whether it managed to avoid the banality of the original dialogue.*

5. **Comparison and reflection:** *Compare the new dialogue with the original and reflect on the differences and improvements made. Consider how you can apply the techniques used in rewriting to other dialogue in your story to eliminate banality and make your dialogue more vivid and engaging.*

This practical exercise will help you develop greater awareness of the traps of banality in dialogues and use effective techniques to make them more interesting and meaningful.

Implied and Unsaid in Dialogues

Using subtext and the unsaid in dialogue can add depth and complexity to your narrative, making character interactions more realistic and engaging. Here are some ways to incorporate implied and unsaid into your dialogue:

1. **Managing unexpressed emotions:** People often do not express all their emotions openly. Use body language, silences and pauses in dialogue to suggest unexpressed emotions. For example, a character might clench their fists or avoid eye contact to hide their anger or discomfort.

2. **Implied responses:** Short or evasive responses may be indicative of emotions or thoughts not expressed openly. For example, instead of answering a question directly, a character might change the subject or give an ambiguous answer to avoid broaching a sensitive topic.

3. **Ambiguous Dialogue:** Create dialogue that leaves room for the reader's interpretation. Use ambiguous phrases or double meanings that can be interpreted in different ways. This can add suspense and mystery to your story, encouraging readers to look for hidden meanings.

4. **Untold Secrets and Suspicions:** Use dialogue to suggest the existence of secrets or suspicions between characters, without explicitly revealing them. For example, a character might make a cryptic comment that suggests he knows something that others don't.

5. **Interrupted Conversations:** Impromptu interruptions or topic changes in dialogue can suggest tension or discomfort between characters. This can be especially effective in times when characters are dealing with emotional conflicts or find themselves in uncomfortable situations.

6. **Whispers and whispers:** Use soft speech or whispers in dialogue to suggest confidentiality or secrecy. This can add an element of suspense and intimacy to character interactions.

7. **Eloquent silence:** Don't underestimate the power of silence in dialogue. Moments of silence can be just as significant as spoken words, suggesting tension, misunderstanding, or deep reflection on the part of the characters.

Incorporating subtext and the unspoken into your dialogue requires sensitivity and attention to detail. However, when used effectively, they can enrich your narrative, adding depth and complexity to character interactions.

Exercise 7: Creating implied dialogues

Objective: Improve the ability to write dialogues that communicate deeper or implicit meanings without directly explaining it.

Exercise steps:

1. **Character and Situation Selection**: Choose two characters and imagine a situation where there is unresolved tension or a shared secret between them.

2. **Identifying subtext**: Define the subtext of the dialogue, which is the implicit or unspoken meaning that the characters want to communicate but do not express overtly.

3. **Writing Dialogue**: Write dialogue between characters, being careful to use ambiguous phrases, double entendres, or allusions to communicate subtext without explicitly revealing it.

4. **Analysis**: After writing the dialogue, analyze it to identify how the subtext manifests itself through the words and actions of the characters. Consider whether the underlying message is clear and whether the dialogue helps create tension or interest in the scene.

5. **Reflection and revision**: Reflect on the dialogue and evaluate whether it effectively communicated the subtext in a subtle and convincing way. Make any necessary changes to improve the clarity or effectiveness of the communicated subtext.

Exercise 8: Interpretation of the unsaid

Objective: Improve the ability to interpret implicit or unspoken meaning in existing dialogues.

Exercise steps:

1. **Dialogue Selection**: Choose existing dialogue from your work in progress or a book you've recently read. Make sure the dialogue contains elements of subtext or unspoken text.

2. **Analysis of the Unsaid**: Analyze the dialogue to identify phrases or expressions that suggest implicit or unspoken meanings. Look for clues in tone of voice,

silences, glances, or other nonverbal cues that could indicate hidden intentions or feelings.

3. ***Interpretation:*** *Reflect on the meaning of what is not said in the context of the dialogue and the story as a whole. Try to understand what emotions, motivations, or secrets might be implied in the dialogue and how they affect the plot or character characterization.*

4. ***Discussion:*** *Share your interpretations with a writing partner, friend, or reading group and compare them with their opinions. Discuss together the meaning of what is not said in the dialogue and how it might influence the reader's perception of the story or characters.*

5. ***Final reflection:*** *Reflect on the exercise and consider how you can apply understanding the unsaid in your future dialogues. Try to incorporate subtly and effectively to enrich your writing and create deeper, more engaging dialogue.*

Eliminate the superfluous

Eliminating the superfluous in the dialogue is essential to maintain a tight *pace* and ensure that each conversation contributes significantly to the plot or the characterization of the characters. Here are some tips on how to do it.

1. **Eliminate repetitions:** Avoid repeating concepts or information already expressed previously in dialogues. If a concept has been clarified once, there is no need to repeat it several times. Keep dialogue concise and efficient, cutting out any unnecessary repetition.

2. **Simplify sentences:** Try to express complex concepts or long descriptions in short, direct sentences. Trim the fat by eliminating unnecessary or redundant words and making sentences more concise and punchy. Also, avoid artificial or pompous language, which can weigh down dialogues.

3. **Be careful of filling devices:** Avoid excessive use of filling devices such as "um", "hey", "you know", etc. These can weigh down the dialogues and slow down their pace. Use filler devices only when necessary to reflect the characters' natural way of speaking.

4. **Maintain coherence:** Make sure that every sentence spoken by the characters has a purpose and consistency with their character and the situation they find themselves in . If a sentence doesn't contribute to the plot or characterization, it may be worth cutting.

5. **Be selective with descriptions:** Limit detailed descriptions in the middle of dialogue. If you need to provide information about settings or characters, do so in a concise and to-the-point way. Too much description can interrupt the flow of the conversation and distract the reader from the dialogue itself.

6. **Avoid didactic speeches:** Avoid having characters give long, didactic speeches that seem more suited to an essay than a realistic conversation. If you must convey important information through dialogue, try to do so in

a natural and integrated way, through lively and meaningful exchanges between characters.

7. **Use silence effectively**: Silence can be just as eloquent as words in dialogue. Use pauses and moments of silence to create suspense, tension, or reflection between characters. This can be especially effective in moments of high tension or emotionally charged dialogue.

Eliminating the superfluous in dialogues requires discipline and a critical evaluation of one's work. But by eliminating the superfluous parts and keeping only what is essential, your dialogues will be more incisive, engaging and memorable.

Exercise 9: Dialogue without empty words

Objective: Improve the ability to write dialogues free of empty words or unnecessary repetitions.

Exercise steps:

1. ***Dialogue Selection****: Choose dialogue from your work in progress or write a new one that features empty words or unnecessary repetition.*

2. ***Dialogue Analysis****: Analyze dialogue to identify empty words or repetitions that could be eliminated without compromising the meaning or flow of communication. Look for phrases or words that add little value to the dialogue or that repeat concepts that have already been clearly expressed.*

3. ***Rewriting without empty words****: Rewrite the dialogue by eliminating empty words and unnecessary*

repetitions. Try to simplify sentences and communicate the message more directly and concisely.

4. **Evaluation**: After rewriting the dialogue, evaluate the quality and effectiveness of the new version. Ask yourself if communication has become clearer and if dialogue is now more fluid and engaging without empty words or unnecessary repetitions.

5. **Comparison and reflection**: Compare the new version of the dialogue with the original and reflect on the differences and the effects of reducing empty words. Consider how this change helped improve the overall quality of the dialogue, and consider how you can apply this technique in your future writing to make the dialogue more effective and engaging.

This exercise will help you develop a greater awareness of the importance of precision and conciseness in dialogue.

Show, don't tell

The principle of "Show, don't tell" is crucial in writing dialogue, allowing readers to experience emotions and situations through the characters' actions and interactions rather than through simple description. Here's how you can develop this principle in your dialogues:

1. **Express emotions through body language**: Rather than directly telling how characters feel, show their emotions through body language. For example, instead of saying, "I was sad," you might describe how the character looks down, shrugs, and bites his or her lower lip.

2. **Use facial expressions and gestures:** Facial expressions and gestures can be powerful indicators of characters' emotions. Describe the grimaces, smiles, sighs, and other gestures that reflect the characters' emotional state during dialogue.

3. **Take advantage of tone of voice:** Tone of voice can convey a lot about your characters' emotions and state of mind. Use tone-of-voice descriptions, such as voice shaking, angry tone, or soft whisper, to emphasize emotion in dialogue.

4. **Describe your surroundings:** Your surroundings can influence the tone and content of your dialogue. Describe the physical context in which the conversation occurs, including sounds, smells and tactile sensations, to create a more vivid and engaging atmosphere.

5. **Pay attention to subtext:** Often what isn't said explicitly is just as important as what is said. Pay attention to subtext in dialogue, that is, hidden meanings or unexpressed tensions between characters.

6. **Avoid Direct Exposure:** Try to avoid directly exposing characters' emotions or intentions through dialogue. Instead, it shows these emotions through the characters' actions, reactions, and unspoken words.

7. **Use internal conflicts:** Dialogue can be fertile ground for exploring characters' internal conflicts. Show doubts, uncertainties and contradictions through the

characters' words and actions, rather than exposing them directly through internal monologue.

8. **Be subtle:** There's no need to emphasize every emotion or detail through dialogue. Be subtle and let readers infer the characters' emotions and intentions through nuances in dialogue and actions.

By using these tips, you can create more vivid, engaging, and meaningful dialogue that shows emotions and situations through the characters' actions and interactions.

Exercise 10: Expressing emotions through actions

Objective: Improve the ability to communicate emotions through actions and behaviors, rather than through explicit statements in dialogues.

Exercise steps:

1. *Choose an emotionally charged situation for your characters, such as an intense argument or a tense moment.*

2. *Write the dialogue that accompanies the scene, but limit direct statements about the emotional state of the characters.*

3. *Instead, focus on the characters' actions and behaviors that suggest their emotions. For example, instead of saying "I'm angry!", describe the character as clenching his fists or tensing up.*

4. *Reread the dialogue and evaluate whether the characters' actions and behaviors effectively convey*

their emotions without the need for explicit statements.

Exercise 11: Use the description of the environment for emotional tone

Objective: Improve your ability to use descriptions of your surroundings to evoke the emotional tone of a scene, rather than stating it directly in dialogue.

Exercise steps:

1. *Choose a scene in which the characters are dealing with an emotionally significant moment, such as a farewell or a turning point in the plot.*

2. *Write dialogue for the scene, but limit direct statements about the characters' emotions.*

3. *Instead, use descriptions of your surroundings to suggest the emotional tone of the scene. For example, describe the stormy sky or the heavy silence in the venue.*

4. *Reread the dialogue along with the description of the setting and evaluate whether the latter effectively helps convey the emotional tone of the scene without the need for direct statements.*

Consistency in language

Maintaining consistency in your dialogue language is essential to creating believable and consistent characters within your story. Here are some tips for making sure your characters' language is consistent and authentic:

1. **Know your characters:** Before writing dialogue, make sure you have a clear understanding of each character's personality, background , and social context. This will

help you determine the type of language that would be natural for them to use.

2. **Develop a distinctive style for each character:** Each character should have their own speaking style, which reflects their personality, their level of education, their social context and their cultural background. For example, an educated and cultured character might use more formal and refined language, while a less educated character might speak in a more simple and direct way.

3. **Pay attention to dialects and regionalisms:** If your characters come from different geographic regions or have different cultural backgrounds , you may want to incorporate dialects or regionalisms into their dialogue. However, be sure to do so in a consistent and respectful manner, avoiding stereotypes or caricatures.

4. **Monitor colloquial language:** Dialogue should sound natural and realistic, but be careful not to overuse slang or jargon that is too specific, especially if it may become obsolete over time. Try to find a balance between authenticity and accessibility for your audience.

5. **Maintain consistency in linguistic register:** Make sure the linguistic register of your characters is consistent with the genre and style of your story. For example, if you're writing a historical novel, the characters should speak in a register appropriate to the era in which the book is set.

6. **Refer to characterization notes:** If you've created detailed character sheets for your characters, use this information to maintain consistency in their language. Review these notes periodically as you write to ensure you stay true to your character's vision.

7. **Revisit dialogue during revision:** During the revision phase, take the time to carefully reread the dialogue to ensure that it is coherent and that the characters' language is appropriate. Edit any dialogue that seems out of place or out of line with the characters' characterization.

Maintaining consistency in your dialogue language requires attention to detail and an in-depth understanding of your characters. Take the time to develop your characters' language consistently and authentically, as this will help make your narrative more believable and engaging for the reader.

Exercise 12: Linguistic characterization sheets

1. *Prepare characterization sheets for each character in your book, including how they speak, words they often*

use, any distinctive expressions or phrases, and their accent, if applicable.

2. Write some short dialogues for each character, trying to maintain consistency in their language and speaking style.

Exercise 13: Exchange of roles

1. Choose two characters from your book with contrasting speaking styles.

2. Write a short conversation in which the two characters exchange their usual speaking roles. For example, if one of the characters is usually formal, have him adopt a more informal speaking style and vice versa.

3. Examine how this role switching affects the dynamics of the conversation and the reader's perception of the characters.

These practice exercises will help you develop a greater awareness of your characters' language and maintain consistency in their speech throughout the book.

Revisit and revision

The phase of revisiting and revising the dialogues is crucial to ensure that they are effective, coherent and impactful. Here are some steps to follow during this process.

1. **Distancing:** After completing the first draft of your dialogues, take some time to distance yourself from your work. Let the manuscript rest for a while, so you can return to it with a fresh, critical eye.

2. **Read aloud:** Reading dialogue aloud can help you identify any issues with flow, pacing, or coherence. Pay

attention to how sentences sound and consider whether they reflect the tone and style of your characters.

3. **Assess pacing:** Check the pace of dialogue, making sure it's well balanced between quicker quips and more thoughtful moments. Avoid letting dialogue become too long or wordy, maintaining a fast pace that holds the reader's attention.

4. **Check character consistency:** Make sure dialogue is consistent with your characters' personalities, backgrounds, and goals. The characters should speak in a way that is consistent with their character and the lifestyle you have outlined for them.

5. **Eliminate repetitions and fillers:** Cut any unnecessary repetitions or fillers that weigh down dialogue. Make sure every sentence and line contributes significantly to the plot or character characterization.

6. **Pay attention to narrative structure and coherence:** Check that dialogue is coherently integrated into the overall plot of the story. Make sure each conversation contributes to the progression of the narrative and that there are no plot holes.

7. **Detect any ambiguity or confusion:** Try to identify any obscure or ambiguous points in the dialogue that could confuse the reader. Clarify any information or

intentions that may not be clear through the characters' words.

8. **Ask beta readers for feedback:** Before writing dialogues off, ask beta readers to read and evaluate the work. Listen to their feedback and consider any suggestions or criticisms that might help you improve the dialogues.

9. **Repeat the revision process:** Repeat the revision process several times, if necessary, until the dialogue is clear, engaging, and consistent with your creative vision for the story.

Reviewing dialogue can take time and dedication, but it is an essential step in ensuring the quality and effectiveness of your storytelling. Pay attention to detail and don't be afraid to make significant changes to improve the overall quality of the dialogue.

Experimenting with narrative voice

Narrative voice is one of the most distinctive characteristics of a literary text. It brings the story to life, conveying the tone, style, and perspective through which the narrative is presented to the reader. Experimenting with narrative voice allows writers to explore new ways to engage the reader and give depth to their narrative. In this chapter, we'll look at different techniques for experimenting with narrative voice and discover which ones work best for your story.

Exploring different narrative voices

Exploring various narrative voices is an excellent way to add depth and complexity to your narrative. Below, we'll explore some techniques for experimenting with different narrator voices:

- **Try first person:** Narrating in first person gives the reader immediate access to the narrator's emotions and thoughts. This approach creates a direct and intimate bond between the reader and the protagonist, allowing you to experience the story through his eyes. Experiment with first person using different tones and writing styles to create unique and authentic narrators.

- **Exploring limited third person:** Limited third-person narration allows you to tell the story from an outside perspective, but focused on a single character. This approach offers greater narrative flexibility than first-person, allowing you to explore multiple points of view within the same story. Experiment with limited third person to deepen the characterization of your characters and to give the reader a broader view of the narrative world.

- **Use the omniscient narrative voice:** The omniscient narrative voice provides the narrator with a complete view of the story and its characters. This approach allows access to the thoughts and emotions of multiple characters, giving the reader a deeper understanding of the internal dynamics of the plot. Explore the omniscient narrative voice to create complex, layered narratives that explore the nuances of the human condition.

Exercise 14: Exploring first-person and third-person narration

Objective: Develop a deeper understanding of the differences between first-person and third-person narration and experiment with both narrative voices.

Exercise steps:

1. *Choose a scene or passage from your story or a literary text that you like.*

2. *Rewrite the scene using first-person narration. Focus on how the change in perspective affects the tone, style, and characterization of the scene.*

3. *Next, rewrite the same scene again using limited third-person narration. Explore how this change in perspective can offer a different view of the characters and events of the story.*

4. *Compare the two versions of the scene and reflect on how the differences in narrative voice affect your perception of the story. Consider which narrative voice best fits the tone and style of your overall narrative.*

This exercise will help you develop a deeper understanding of narrative voices and experiment with different perspectives to improve your writing.

Playing with style and tone

Experimenting with storytelling style and tone is an effective way to give your story personality and depth. Here are some strategies for playing with narrative style and tone:

- **Explore different writing styles:** Experiment with a variety of writing styles, from formal to conversational, descriptive to minimalist. Each style has its own uniqueness and can greatly influence the reading experience. For example, formal language can lend an aura of authority and tradition to your narrative, while a conversational style can make the story more accessible and close to the reader.

- **Adjust the narrative tone:** The narrative tone can vary from humorous to serious, from playful to dark. Choose the tone that best suits your story and its themes, and experiment with small accents to create unique and engaging atmospheres. For example, using an ironic or sarcastic style can bring lightness to a narrative, while a darker, more dramatic tone can increase the tension and emotion of the story.

Exercise 15: Experiment with narrative style and tone

Objective: Develop the ability to manipulate narrative style and tone to achieve desired effects in storytelling.

Exercise steps:

1. *Choose a scene from your story or a literary text you like.*

2. *Rewrite the scene using a different writing style than the original. For example, if the scene was originally written in a descriptive, formal style, try rewriting it using a more conversational, lively style.*

3. *Next, rewrite the same scene again using a different narrative tone. For example, if the scene was*

originally written in a serious, thoughtful tone, try rewriting it using a lighter, more humorous tone.

4. *Compare different versions of the scene and think about how narrative style and tone affect your perception of the story. Consider what combination of style and tone best suits the message and spirit of your narrative.*

This exercise will help you explore the different possibilities offered by manipulating narrative style and tone, allowing you to find the perfect combination for your story.

Explore different perspectives

Exploring various narrative perspectives can enrich your story, giving the reader a more complete and nuanced view of events and characters. Here are some strategies for exploring different perspectives:

- **Try alternative points of view:** In addition to the traditional points of view of the protagonists, consider telling the story from alternative perspectives. This could include the perspectives of secondary characters, antagonists, or outside observers. Exploring different perspectives can add depth and complexity to your narrative, allowing you to explore otherwise overlooked aspects of the story.

- **Use collective voice:** Collective voice is a narrative technique in which a group of characters or a community narrates the story as a collective entity. This approach can offer a unique perspective on the story and social dynamics of the characters, allowing the reader to see events through the eyes of an entire group. Explore the collective voice to create choral narratives that explore the complexity of human relationships and social conflicts.

Exercise 16: Exploring alternative points of view

Objective: Develop the ability to explore alternative points of view and experiment with unconventional narrative perspectives.

Exercise steps:

1. *Choose a scene from your story or a literary text you like.*

2. *Rewrite the scene using the point of view of a secondary character or an outside observer. Pay attention to how this new perspective changes your perception of events and characters.*

3. *Next, try rewriting the same scene again using the collective voice. Imagine that a group of characters are narrating the story together, sharing their experiences and points of view. Explore how this collective perspective changes the narrative and understanding of history.*

4. *Compare different versions of the scene and consider how exploring alternative points of view can enrich your narrative. Consider how these new perspectives might be integrated into your story to give the reader a fuller, more nuanced view of the events and characters.*

This exercise will help you develop the ability to explore alternative points of view and experiment with unconventional narrative perspectives, enriching your writing and offering the reader a richer, more engaging narrative.

Experimenting with narrative voice is a creative and inspiring process that can lead to surprising discoveries and enrich your writing. Don't be afraid to explore new territory and find the narrative voice that best suits your story and personal style. Remember that consistent practice and openness to exploration are key to growing and improving as a writer.

Chapter three

Plot Development and Planning

"Planning a story is like sailing on the open sea. You have to chart a course, but you also have to be ready to adapt to unexpected waves."

JK ROWLING

Plot development and planning are key to creating an engaging, well-structured story. In this chapter, we'll look at different techniques and strategies for creating compelling plots to capture the reader's attention and hold it until the end of the story, work with the narrative arc, and address creative blocks during the writing process.

Create compelling, well-structured plots

The plot of a story is its supporting skeleton, the common thread that holds the events and characters together. To create a compelling and well-structured plot, it is important to carefully plan the key elements of the story, including the incipit, development and conflict resolution.

Identify the main conflict

Identifying the main conflict is a critical step in creating a compelling and engaging plot. Conflict is the beating heart of the story, the engine that drives the action forward and creates narrative tension. In this process, it is essential to delve into the concept of conflict in all its facets and complexities.

Conflict is not simply a struggle between good and evil, but can manifest itself in multiple forms and levels of depth. It could be a character's internal conflict, their internal struggles, doubts, conflicting desires, or external conflict, such as clashes with other characters, environmental obstacles, or adverse situations. This conflict can arise from a wide range of sources: from the characters' personal ambitions to external forces that threaten their world.

To make it engaging, the main conflict must be clear, relevant, and meaningful to the characters and the development of the plot. It must represent a significant challenge that the characters must face and overcome to achieve their goals or resolve their dilemmas. Furthermore, the conflict should have deep emotional and psychological implications for the characters, offering them the opportunity to grow and develop over the course of the story.

It is also important to consider the evolution of the conflict throughout history. The main conflict should develop and intensify as the plot unfolds, leading to new challenges, changes in character relationships, and unexpected turns in the narrative. This ensures that the conflict always remains relevant and engaging for the reader, maintaining attention and fueling interest until the story's conclusion.

In summary, identifying the main conflict requires a thorough understanding of the nuances of the narrative and character motives. It's an essential process for creating a compelling, engaging plot that keeps the reader glued to the pages of your book.

Exercise 17: Deepen the main conflict

Objective: Develop the ability to identify and explore the main conflict within a story.

Exercise steps:

1. *Choose a story you have recently read or are currently writing and identify the main conflict. This could be a character's internal conflict or an external conflict that manifests itself through character interactions or plot events.*

2. *Write a brief description of the main conflict, including its main protagonists, the nature of the conflict, and its implications for the plot and the characters involved.*

3. *Make a list of at least three key events or situations in the story that are directly influenced or caused by the main conflict. These could be tense moments, character clashes, or significant plot twists.*

4. *Consider how the main conflict influences the behavior and actions of the characters in the story. Write a brief analysis of the ways in which conflict contributes to character development and plot progression.*

5. *Consider how you could delve further into the main conflict to make the story more compelling and engaging for the reader. Consider introducing new facets of conflict, adding new obstacles for characters, or developing unexpected twists in the narrative.*

Working with the narrative arc

Working with the narrative arc is essential for building a compelling and well-structured story. This arc represents the emotional and thematic journey that runs through the narrative, characterized by conflict, action and resolution. Having already analyzed the conflict, we focus on the other two elements.

Action

Action in a narrative is not just about breathtaking chase or battle sequences, but rather the set of events and situations that advance the plot and maintain the reader's interest. Here are some tips for effectively developing action in a story:

1. **Meaningful character choices:** The characters' actions must be meaningful and consistent with their characterization. Each choice should have consequences that influence the direction of the story and the development of the characters themselves. Rather than simple random events, actions should be the result of the characters' motivations, desires, and conflicts.

2. **Tension Progression:** The narrative should be structured to progressively increase tension. This can be achieved by introducing obstacles that are increasingly difficult to overcome, revealing crucial information at the right time, or placing characters faced with impossible choices. The growing tension

keeps the reader engaged and eager to know what will happen next.

3. **Narrative Revelations and Turns:** Narrative turns and significant revelations maintain the reader's interest and move the plot forward. These moments can include unexpected plot twists, new information that changes the meaning of previous events, or emotional turns that transform the characters' perspectives. Revelations should be well integrated into the plot and have a significant impact on the direction of the story.

4. **Balance between action and reflection:** It is important to find a balance between action scenes and moments of reflection and emotional exploration. Action scenes can be engaging and thought-provoking, but it's also important to give characters time to process events and reflect on their experiences. This allows the reader to connect emotionally with the characters and better understand their motivations and changes.

5. **Variation in pace:** Alternate action scenes with other types of scenes to keep the pace of the narrative interesting and engaging. Calm moments can be used to deepen relationships between characters, explore themes, or provide information crucial to the plot. This variation in pace keeps the reader engaged and prevents them from getting tired of the constant action sequences.

Effectively developing the action in a story requires a combination of planning, revision, and attention to detail. It's important to balance the suspense and emotion of action scenes with coherence of characters and plot progression. When done with care, action can transform an ordinary story into an unforgettable adventure for the reader.

Resolution

The resolution is the culmination of the story arc, the point at which the main conflict is resolved satisfactorily. It is the moment when the key questions of the story are answered and the reader's expectations are met. Here are some elements to consider to effectively develop the resolution of a story:

1. **Closing Narrative Threads:** The resolution should close all major narrative threads that have been introduced throughout the story. This means providing answers to questions posed by the reader, clarifying unsolved mysteries, and bringing all major plots to a satisfying conclusion.

2. **Emotional Satisfaction:** The resolution should provide emotional satisfaction for both the characters and the reader. This can include moments of growth and change for characters, reconciliations between conflicting characters, and the realization of the protagonists' goals. It's important that the resolution

feels natural and consistent with the development of the story.

3. **Avoid solutions that are too convenient:** It is important to avoid solutions that seem too easy or conventional. The resolution should be the result of the characters' actions and the choices they have made throughout the story. This makes the resolution more believable and satisfying for the reader.

4. **Open space for the future:** Even if the main plot is resolved, the resolution can also open up new possibilities for the future. This might include introducing new challenges or conflicts, promising new adventures for the characters, or suggesting how they might continue their lives after the story ends.

5. **Conclusion consistent with the themes:** The resolution should be consistent with the themes and issues addressed in the story. For example, if the story dealt with themes of forgiveness and redemption, the resolution might focus on moments of reconciliation and personal growth for the characters involved.

Developing an effective resolution requires careful planning and a thorough understanding of the story's themes and characters. It is the culminating moment that leaves the reader with a lasting impression and a feeling of emotional and narrative closure. A well-executed resolution can turn a good story into an unforgettable experience for the reader.

To successfully work on the narrative arc, it is important to balance these three elements in order to maintain the pace and interest of the reader throughout the story. The conflict should be consistent and meaningful, the action should be engaging, and the resolution should be satisfying and consistent with the tone and themes of the story.

Furthermore, it is important to note that the narrative arc is not necessarily linear. It can be shaped into various forms, such as the traditional arc (introduction, development, climax, resolution), or it can be more subtle and subtle, with twists and climaxes distributed unconventionally throughout the course of the story.

Developing an effective narrative arc requires planning, revision, and constant attention to the coherence and cohesion of the narrative. It's a fundamental element of creative writing that can take a story from good to great.

The non-traditional narrative arc

Non-traditional arcs offer a creative and innovative way to structure a story. In contrast to the conventional approach, in which the plot follows a linear path from introduction to climax and resolution, non-traditional story arcs can be more subtle, complex, and often challenging for the reader. Here are some examples of non-traditional story arcs and how they can be developed:

1. **Circular narrative arc:** the story ends where it began, creating a sense of cyclicality and return. This can be

used to explore themes of fate, rebirth or repetition. The key to developing this type of narrative arc is to create a meaningful connection between the beginning and end of the story, revealing how characters and situations have changed or evolved over time.

2. **Non-Linear Narrative Arc:** The plot does not necessarily follow a linear chronological path. It may include flashbacks, flashforwards, or time jumps that give the reader an unconventional perspective on the story. Developing this type of arc requires careful planning and a clear understanding of how each event connects to the others to create a coherent and meaningful narrative.

3. **Mosaic Story Arc:** The story is made up of a series of vignettes or fragments that together form a larger picture. This approach can be used to explore a variety of points of view or experiences, giving the reader a multiple perspective on the story. Developing a mosaic narrative arc requires the ability to skillfully weave together different voices and perspectives to create a cohesive and engaging picture.

4. **Narrative arc with multiple parallel plots:** the story unfolds through several parallel plots that intersect and influence each other. This can create a sense of complexity and connection between different characters and their stories. Developing a narrative arc with multiple parallel plots requires effective

management of characters and their relationships, as well as careful planning to ensure that all plots develop in a coherent and meaningful way.

5. **Unresolved Story Arc:** The story ends without a clear or definitive conclusion. This can be used to create a sense of mystery or ambiguity, inviting the reader to reflect on the meaning of the story and the fate of the characters. Developing this type of arc requires subtlety in balancing the reader's suspense and frustration, while leaving enough room for personal interpretation and reflection.

Developing non-traditional story arcs can be a challenge, but it also offers the opportunity to explore new forms and structure stories in unique and surprising ways. The key is to find a balance between innovation and narrative coherence, creating a narrative that is inspiring and meaningful to the reader.

Nontraditional story arcs give writers the freedom to experiment with story structure and presentation in innovative and surprising ways. Here are some features and tips for working with unconventional story arcs:

1. **Nonlinear Structure:** In a nontraditional story arc, the story does not necessarily follow a linear structure with a beginning, middle, and conclusion. Instead, it can be organized in a non-linear way, with flashbacks, time jumps, or fragmented narratives that reveal information non-chronologically. This can create a sense of

suspense and mystery, encouraging the reader to make connections between seemingly unrelated events.

2. **Multiple Perspectives:** Another non-traditional approach is to use multiple perspectives to tell the story. This may mean alternating between the points of view of different characters or using narrative formats such as diaries, letters or audio recordings to offer a more complete and nuanced view of events.

3. **Epistolary-Style Narration:** A non-traditional story arc can be constructed using epistolary-style narration, in which the story is told through letters, emails, text messages, or other means of communication. This approach can add an element of authenticity and intimacy to the narrative, allowing readers to enter directly into the characters' thoughts and feelings.

4. **Circular Structure:** Some unconventional story arcs adopt a circular structure, in which the story returns to its starting point at the end. This can be used to emphasize recurring themes or to create a sense of cycle or recurrence in the narrative.

5. **Nonverbal Fiction:** Some authors choose to explore nontraditional narrative arcs through nonverbal forms, such as comics, graphic design, theater, or film. These mediums allow writers to make the most of the power of imagery and symbolism to tell complex, engaging stories.

Exercise 18: Exploring a non-traditional narrative arc

Objective: Develop the ability to experiment with unconventional narrative forms to create original and engaging stories.

Exercise steps:

1. Choose a concept or story idea you're interested in exploring using a nontraditional story arc. For example, you may want to tell a story using flashbacks, multiple perspectives, or a circular structure.

2. Choose the narrative format that best suits your story. It could be a novel, a short story, a series of vignettes, or any other format that inspires you.

3. Experiment with the structure and presentation of your story. Play with the order of events, explore different perspectives, and consider how you might incorporate nonverbal elements into your narrative.

4. Reflect on the challenges and opportunities presented by using a nontraditional story arc. What did you learn from the experimentation process? What surprised or inspired you?

5. Review and refine your work based on the feedback you receive. Ask readers from different backgrounds to weigh in on your story and offer opinions on its emotional and narrative impact.

This exercise will help you develop your creativity and explore new narrative forms that can enrich your stories and engage your readers in new and surprising ways.

Methods for planning a story

Planning a story is a crucial step for writers, as it provides structure and guidance during the writing process. There are several planning methods that authors can use, each with their own benefits and challenges. Here are some of the most common ways to plan a story:

1. **Outline:** This is one of the more traditional planning methods, where you create a detailed document that outlines the story's major events, turning points, key characters, and other significant elements. The outline can be structured hierarchically, with chapters, scenes and subsections, or it can be more free and flexible.

2. **Mind Map:** This planning method uses visual diagrams to represent the relationships between different story elements. You start with a central concept (such as a main idea or key event) and create branches that branch out in various directions, representing characters, subplots, themes, and other narrative elements. Mind maps can be particularly useful for exploring connections between different parts of the story and for generating new ideas.

3. **Directions on slides or cards:** This method involves writing short descriptions or key points on digital slides or physical cards. Each slide or card represents a specific element of the story, such a scene, character, or theme, and can be easily organized,

manipulated, and rearranged to explore different narrative structures and event sequences.

4. **Plot Diagram:** A plot diagram is a graphic display of the story's narrative structure, showing the flow of conflict, action, and resolution. It can be presented as a linear timeline, with peaks and valleys representing moments of tension and resolution, or as a more complex diagram showing the interconnections between different narrative threads.

5. **Script or storyboard:** This method is especially useful for writers working on visual projects such as films or comics. It involves creating a series of panels or scenes that represent the events of the story in sequential order. This helps authors visualize plot progression and plan the pace and flow of the narrative.

6. **Organic or "pantser" approach (without detailed planning):** Some authors prefer to start writing without detailed planning, going with the flow of creativity and letting the story develop naturally during the writing process. This approach can be liberating and inspiring, but it can also lead to challenges of coherence and structure.

Choosing the right planning method depends on the author's personal style, the complexity of the story, and individual preferences. Some authors may find it useful to combine multiple methods, for example using a detailed outline together with a mind map to explore ideas and connections.

The important thing is to find an approach that works for you and helps you organize your ideas and develop a coherent, compelling story.

Exercise 19: Exploring planning with a mind map

Objective: Use a mind map to explore and organize key ideas for a story.

Exercise steps:

1. *Choose a story idea or concept that you are interested in exploring. It could be a general idea for a plot, an interesting character, or a theme you want to develop.*

2. *Take a sheet of paper or use mind mapping software to create a mind map. In the center of the paper, write the main concept or idea for your story.*

3. *From this central idea, start creating branches that branch outward, representing different elements of your story. For example, you might have branches for main characters, subplots, plot turning points, key themes, and other narrative elements.*

4. *For each branch, add details and sub-branches that further expand the ideas. For example, under the main characters branch, you could list their defining traits, their goals, and their relationships with other characters.*

5. *Explore the connections and relationships between the different elements of your mind map. Try to find ways to integrate the different narrative threads and to create a meaningful interconnection between the various aspects of the story.*

6. *Once you've completed your mind map, take some time to review it and reflect on the ideas you've*

generated. Identify the strengths of your story and identify any areas that may need further development.

7. *Use your mind map as a guide during the process of writing your story. It can serve as a reference point for keeping track of characters, plots, and themes, and can help you maintain coherence and cohesion in your narrative.*

This exercise will help you explore your story ideas in a visual and organized way, allowing you to get a comprehensive overview of different narrative elements and plan your story more effectively.

Resolve creative blocks and overcome the impasse in writing

Dealing with creative blocks and impasses during the writing process is a common challenge for writers at all experience levels. However, there are several strategies you can adopt to overcome these obstacles and get back to your creative business.

If you feel stuck on a particular aspect of the story, try changing your perspective. You can write from a different point of view, explore a subplot, or focus on a different character to gain a new perspective and unlock new ideas.

If you feel like you've hit a brick wall, take a break. Let your mind relax and distract itself with other activities. Often, solutions to creative problems emerge when you least expect them, so give yourself the time and space to let your creativity flow.

Free writing, or automatic writing, is an exercise in which you write freely, without worrying about grammar or coherence. This can help clear your mind and generate new ideas, allowing your creativity to flow freely.

Look for inspiration from different sources, such as books, films, music, art or nature. Explore new places, go for walks, visit museums or attend cultural events to fuel your imagination and find new ideas for your story.

If you feel stuck on the plot or details of your story, do a little research and planning. You might explore new topics related to your story, research historical places or periods, or create a detailed outline to help clarify the direction of your narrative.

Talk to other writers, participate in critique groups, or find a writing partner to share your ideas with and get feedback . Interaction with other authors can be a valuable source of support, inspiration, and constructive feedback.

Sometimes, despite all your efforts, you may simply find it difficult to move forward with a particular part of your story. If so, accept the impasse and move on to another part of the story that inspires you more. You can always go back later and tackle the hard part with a fresh perspective.

Remember that creative blocks are a normal part of the creative process and that it's important to be kind to yourself during these trying times. With patience, determination, and a good dose of creativity, you can overcome obstacles and return to your writing with new energy and inspiration.

Chapter four

Characterization and Development of Characters

A good character can make a story memorable, but a great character can make a story everlasting."

JOHN GREEN

In the vast landscape of creative writing, there is one element that stands out for its importance and influence: characters. They are the ones who bring stories to life, who make them tangible, exciting, and unforgettable. In the depths of each narrative, the nuances of their psychology, the intrigues of their relationships and the transformations that shape them over the course of events are hidden. This chapter, dedicated to the characterization and development of characters, aims to explore the art of creating figures that capture the reader's imagination, that arouse empathy, curiosity, and emotional involvement.

In the pages that follow, we'll dive into the creative process behind building vivid, complex characters. We will explore the psychology of the characters, delving into the recesses of their minds to understand their motivations, their internal conflicts and their deepest hopes. We will create detailed sheets that trace the journey of each character, outlining their physical appearance, their background and their relationships with the other protagonists of the story. We will use flashbacks and analepsis to reveal the secrets of their past and to deepen our understanding of their paths of growth and change. And finally, we will explore the concept of arcuate and dynamic characters, analyzing the transformations that make them richer and more multifaceted over the course of the narrative.

Through examples, practical suggestions and creative exercises, we will try to convey the skills and knowledge necessary to create characters that come to life on the page and remain imprinted in the reader's memory. Whether you're writing a novel, a short story, or any other form of storytelling, we hope this chapter provides you with the tools and inspiration you need to create unforgettable characters who thrill, inspire, and intrigue anyone who ventures into your stories.

Delve into the psychology of the characters

Each character is a complex universe of emotions, desires, fears and contradictions, and understanding their psychology is essential to bringing them to life on the page.

Exploring the deep motivations

Motivations are what drives characters to act, make choices, and pursue their goals, and understanding these internal forces is essential to making their behavior and actions believable.

To explore the deeper motivations of your characters, it's important to go beyond superficial reasons and discover what lies at the heart of their actions. This means asking not only what the characters want to achieve, but also why they want it. What are their deepest aspirations, their most intimate desires? What moves them, pushes them forward, keeps them awake at night?

Characters' motivations can arise from a variety of sources, including past experiences, personal relationships, basic needs, and core values. For example, one character might be motivated by a search for love and acceptance due to a difficult childhood, while another might be driven by a thirst for revenge following a betrayal. Exploring these deep motivations can help you better understand characters' actions and make them more coherent and meaningful within the story.

An effective way to explore characters' deep motivations is to ask them deep, provocative questions. For example, you might ask them what they would do if they had all the power in the world, or what they would sacrifice to get what they want most. The answers to these questions can reveal a lot about the psychology of the characters and the forces that drive them.

Additionally, you can explore characters' motivations through analyzing their behavior and actions. Observe how your characters respond to the challenges and conflicts they face, and try to spot recurring patterns in their behavior. This can help you identify their underlying motivations and better understand what drives them.

Finally, it is important to remember that characters' motivations can change throughout the story, in response to the events and experiences they go through. This allows your characters to grow and evolve over the course of the narrative, making them more realistic and dynamic. Exploring your characters' deep motivations is an ongoing, evolving process that can greatly enrich your storytelling and make your characters more vivid and compelling.

Exploring emotional complexity

Exploring the emotional complexity of characters is a crucial element in making their experiences and interactions more realistic and engaging. Each character is a unique blend of emotions, which manifest themselves in a wide range of shades and intensities. To fully capture this emotional complexity, it is essential to consider several dimensions:

1. **Range of Emotions:** Characters should not be monolithic in their emotional state. As humans, they are susceptible to a wide range of emotions, ranging from joyful to sad, courageous to fearful. Exploring this full range of emotions can make your characters more vivid and realistic, allowing them to react authentically to the challenges and triumphs they encounter along their journey.

2. **Origins of Emotions:** Characters' emotions are often rooted in their past experiences, relationships, and personal values. For example, a character might react with anger due to an injustice suffered in the past, or he might feel joy in achieving an important goal. Exploring the origins of your characters' emotions can help you better understand their psychology and give depth to their development.

3. **Contradictions and Ambiguities:** Human emotions are often complex and contradictory, and characters should reflect this ambiguity. For example, a character might have mixed feelings toward another person, such as love and resentment, or might be torn between fear and a desire for change. Exploring these contradictions can make your characters more human and interesting, and can add tension and suspense to your story.

4. **Expression of Emotions:** In addition to exploring your characters' emotions, it's important to consider how these emotions manifest themselves in their behavior, actions, and interactions with other characters. For example, one character might hide their emotions behind a mask of apparent calm, while another might explode into heated confrontation when feeling threatened. Exploring the expression of emotions can help you make your characters more vivid and believable, and can add depth to your storytelling.

Exploring the emotional complexity of characters requires sensitivity and attention to detail. Investing time and energy in creating emotionally rich, multi-faceted characters can lead to more engaging and compelling stories that capture the reader's attention and touch their hearts.

Analyze contradictions and internal conflicts

Analyzing the contradictions and internal conflicts of characters is a key element to making them more realistic, complex and interesting. The contradictions and internal conflicts add depth and tension to the psychology of the characters, as they reflect the complexities of human nature and the internal challenges that each individual faces. Here are some key points to consider:

1. **Contradictions in Values and Beliefs:** Characters may find themselves in conflict between what they believe and what they do in practice. For example, they may uphold certain moral values, but be forced to violate them to achieve an important goal. These contradictions can generate significant internal conflicts and test the moral coherence of the characters.

2. **Conflict Between Conflicting Desires:** Characters may also find themselves in conflict between conflicting or opposing desires. For example, they may crave love and independence at the same time, finding themselves

caught in a conflict between the desire for closeness and the need for freedom. These conflicts can generate great emotional tension and make characters more realistic and human.

3. **Conflicts Between Mixed Emotions:** Characters can experience mixed or conflicting emotions at the same time. For example, they might feel love and hate towards the same person, or joy and sadness towards the same situation. These emotional conflicts can create palpable emotional intensity and make character interactions more complex and engaging.

4. **Conflicts Between Needs and Obligations:** Characters may also find themselves in conflict between their personal needs and their obligations to others. For example, they may want to pursue their dreams, but feel forced to follow a different path to meet family or society's expectations. These conflicts can generate a sense of internal struggle and add depth to character characterization.

Analyzing the contradictions and internal conflicts of the characters requires a deep understanding of their psychology and their motivations. Exploring these elements can help create richer, more multidimensional characters, whose development and growth throughout the story resonate with authenticity and emotional resonance.

Create three-dimensional characters

Creating three-dimensional characters is a fundamental goal for any writer who wants to make their stories engaging and memorable. A three-dimensional character is one who appears as a complex, realistic, and vibrant figure, with multiple layers of personality, emotions, and motivations. Here are some approaches to creating three-dimensional characters:

1. **Personality Complexity:** Avoid clichés and flat characters that fit simple stereotypes. Instead, develop characters who display a wide range of personality traits, with nuances and contradictions that make them human and believable. Consider how different aspects of their personality interact with each other and how they manifest themselves in their actions and interactions with other characters.

2. **Motivations and Goals:** Each character should have clear goals and deep motivations that guide their actions and choices. However, make their motivations complex and multifaceted, rather than simple and linear. Explore what your characters truly want and what they are willing to do to get it, even if that means facing internal conflicts or making difficult decisions.

3. **Background and Personal History:** A character's background and personal history have a significant impact on their psychology and actions. Consider what past experiences have shaped your character and how

these experiences influence their current behavior. It uses flashbacks and dialogue to reveal details of their past and to deepen the reader's understanding of their lives and motivations.

4. **Development over the course of the story:** Characters should show some form of development or growth over the course of the story. This can be highlighted through their resolution of conflicts, the transformation of their beliefs, or the change in their relationships with other characters. Make sure your character faces significant challenges and that their experiences have a tangible impact on their personal development.

5. **Interpersonal Relationships:** Relationships between characters are a key element in creating three-dimensional characters. Explore the dynamics of their relationships with other characters and how these relationships influence their development and growth. Consider how your characters react to other characters and how these interactions reveal further details about their personalities and motivations.

Creating three-dimensional characters takes time, dedication, and a deep understanding of human psychology. However, investing in delving deeper into your characters can lead to more engaging and meaningful stories that leave a lasting impression on readers.

Exercise 20: Write a letter from your character's point of view

This exercise will help you get inside your character's mind and explore their psychology from an internal perspective. Choose one of your main characters and imagine you are them for a moment. Write a letter (or diary) from your character to another character, to themselves, or to a fictional character. In the letter, encourage your character to explore their deepest feelings, thoughts, and desires. It speaks of their hopes and fears, their joys and sorrows, their desires and ambitions. Make sure your character opens up completely and expresses himself freely, without limits or restrictions.

After completing the letter, take time to read it and reflect on what you wrote. What did you learn about your character? Are there any new facets of their personality that you have discovered? How will you influence their development in the story based on this new information?

This exercise will help you dig deeper into the psychology of your characters and develop a richer, more detailed understanding of their thoughts and feelings.

Create detailed character sheets

Creating detailed character sheets is a fundamental step to fully understand who your protagonists are, what their motivations are, their distinctive traits and their evolution over the course of the story. Here are some elements you could include in your character sheets:

1. **Basic Information**: Start with basic information about your character, such as name, age, physical appearance, and cultural background . These details will provide a foundation on which to build the rest of the board.

2. **Personality and Traits:** Describe your character's personality and the traits that make them unique. What makes them happy? What bothers them? What are their strengths and weaknesses?

3. **Goals and Motivations:** Identify your character's main goals and their motivations for achieving them. What is their greatest wish? What motivates them to fight for what they want?

4. **Background and Personal History:** Provide details about your character's background and personal history. What experiences have shaped who I am today? What were the most significant moments of their lives?

5. **Interpersonal Relationships:** Explore your character's relationships with other characters in the story. Who are the most important people in their life? What are the dynamics of their relationships?

6. **Challenges and Conflicts:** Identify the major challenges and conflicts your character faces throughout the story. What are their main obstacles? How do they react when faced with difficulties?

7. **Development over the course of the story:** Predict how your character might develop and change over the course of the story. What are the lessons they will learn? How will they grow and transform through their experiences?

Creating detailed character sheets will help you maintain a clear vision of your protagonists and develop them consistently and convincingly throughout the story. Be sure to refer to character sheets as you write, to ensure your characters stay true to their original vision and develop organically and realistically.

At this point, having now acquired all the tools to characterize a character, it is worth recalling the example given in the first chapter on Harry Potter:

Name: Harry James Potter
Ages: 11-17 (over the course of the books in the series)
Physical Appearance: Black hair, green eyes, wears round glasses. Slim but athletic build. He bears a lightning bolt-shaped scar on his forehead.
Background and Personal History: Harry was born on July 31, 1980, the son of James and Lily Potter, two wizards who were killed by Lord Voldemort when Harry was just a child. He grew up with his aunt and uncle, the Dursleys, who treated him badly and hid his true identity as a wizard until his eleventh birthday, when he received his acceptance letter to Hogwarts.
Personality and distinctive traits: Harry is brave, loyal and altruistic, but often impulsive and stubborn. He has great compassion for others and a well-developed sense of justice. However, he can also be very resentful and distrustful of those he believes he cannot trust.
Goals and Motivations: Harry's primary desire is to defeat Lord Voldemort and end his tyranny. He is motivated by his determination to do the right thing and protect those he loves,

especially his closest friends, Hermione Granger and Ron Weasley.

Interpersonal relationships: Harry has a very close relationship with his friends at Hogwarts, especially Hermione and Ron, with whom he shares numerous adventures and dangers. He also has a complex relationship with his mentor, Albus Dumbledore, and an antagonistic relationship with his enemy, Draco Malfoy .

Challenges and Conflicts: Harry faces numerous challenges along his journey, including the fight against Voldemort and his followers, as well as the sense of isolation and alienation he often feels due to his celebrity and his scar.

Development Over the Course of the Story: Over the course of the series, Harry grows and matures considerably. He learns to trust his friends, accept help from others and make sacrifices for the greater good. Ultimately, he becomes a courageous and selfless leader, willing to sacrifice his own life to protect others.

This sheet provides an overview of the main features of Harry Potter, allowing authors to fully understand who the character is and how he evolves over the course of the series.

Use flashbacks and analepsis to develop the characters' story

Using flashbacks and analepsis is a valuable narrative technique that allows writers to delve deeper into characters' histories, offering a richer understanding of their motives, past traumas, and relationships. These techniques can reveal significant details about characters' pasts, integrating them organically with the narrative flow. It is crucial that these revelations are strategically inserted into the narrative, so as to be relevant to the overall plot of the story and the development of the characters in the present. Flashbacks should have a clear narrative purpose, contributing to the overall theme of the story or character characterization. It is important to balance the use of flashbacks and analepsis, avoiding overloading the narrative with superfluous information. When executed with care and skill, these tools can enrich storytelling, giving readers a deeper and more engaging insight into characters and their stories.

Reveal the characters' pasts

Revealing characters' pasts through flashbacks and analepsis is a valuable opportunity for writers to add depth and complexity to plot and characterization. These techniques allow readers to immerse themselves in characters' past experiences, offering a richer understanding of their motives, traumas, and relationships.

A crucial aspect in revealing the past of the characters is the choice of when and how this revelation occurs. Flashbacks should be inserted strategically into the narrative, so that they integrate organically with the flow of the story and provide relevant information at the right time. For example, a flashback could be used to explain a character's present behavior, providing emotional or psychological context for their actions.

It is also essential to consider how the characters' pasts influence their development and growth over the course of the story. Characters' past experiences can have a lasting impact on their personalities and relationships, and revealing these experiences through flashbacks and analepsis can provide the reader with a fuller perspective on their changes over time. For example, showing a key event from a character's past could illuminate their motivations or emotional journey in the present.

Furthermore, it is important that revelations about the characters' pasts are meaningful and relevant to the overall plot of the story. Each flashback should have a clear narrative purpose, contributing to the overall theme of the story or character characterization. For example, a flashback might reveal a previously hidden secret that changes the course of events or challenges the main characters' beliefs.

Finally, it is essential to balance the amount of flashbacks and analepsis used in the story, avoiding overloading the narrative with superfluous information or slowing down the pace of the story. Authors should be selective in their use of these techniques, ensuring that each revelation about the past contributes significantly to the overall understanding of the characters and plot.

Ultimately, revealing characters' pasts through flashbacks and analepsis is a delicate art that requires narrative sensitivity and an intuition for the right moment. When done with care and skill, this technique can enrich the narrative, giving readers a deeper and more engaging insight into the characters and their stories.

Provide historical context

Providing historical context through flashbacks and analepsis is an essential aspect of storytelling that allows writers to situate the story within a specific time period and show how past events have influenced the characters' present. This technique allows readers to better understand the world of the story and appreciate the cultural, social, and historical influences that have shaped the characters and events.

One of the main advantages of using flashbacks and analepsis to provide historical context is that it allows authors to show rather than tell. Rather than simply providing information through direct narration, flashbacks allow readers to directly see past events and their consequences. For example, rather than describing a historical event through an explanatory speech, a flashback can directly show the characters experiencing that event, making the narrative more engaging and tangible.

Additionally, providing historical context through flashbacks and analepsis allows authors to explore the causes and effects of past events on the story and characters. Authors can show how decisions made in the past have influenced the present and how certain historical patterns or themes repeat themselves throughout history. This approach gives readers a broader perspective and greater understanding of the complexity of the characters and events.

However, it is important to use these techniques sparingly and discerningly. Too many flashbacks or analepsis can interrupt the narrative flow and distract readers from the main plot. Authors should be selective in their use of these techniques, inserting flashbacks strategically and ensuring that any past revelations are relevant and significant to the overall plot of the story.

In conclusion, providing historical context through flashbacks and analepsis is an important narrative technique that enriches the narrative, giving readers a more in-depth and engaging insight into the story world and its characters. Used with care and skill, this technique can enhance readers' understanding and appreciation of the story, creating a richer, more immersive reading experience.

Create suspense and mystery

One of the main ways to create suspense and mystery is to reveal crucial information through flashbacks and analepsis at key moments in the narrative. These revelations can upset the reader's expectations, revealing new information that radically changes the perception of the story or characters. For example, a flashback might reveal a well-kept secret that calls into question everything the characters and readers thought they knew up until that point.

Furthermore, the use of flashbacks and analepsis can create suspense through the manipulation of narrative time. Authors can jump back and forth in time, creating a non-linear narrative structure that keeps readers on the edge of their seats, eager to discover how events will evolve in the present. This temporal discontinuity can generate a sense of uncertainty and anticipation, fueling the desire to discover how all the pieces of the puzzle fit together.

Finally, creating suspense and mystery through flashbacks and analepsis requires a delicate balance between revelation and delay of gratification. The authors must carefully dose the information revealed through flashbacks and analepsis, keeping some cards hidden to keep the suspense and the reader's interest alive until the end. This means avoiding revealing key plot secrets too early and maintaining a constant narrative tension that keeps readers on the edge of their seats until the last page.

Ultimately, creating suspense and mystery through flashbacks and analepsis is an effective narrative technique that keeps readers glued to the pages and keeps them reading to find out what happens next. Used skillfully, this technique can make storytelling more engaging and exciting, offering readers an unforgettable and compelling reading experience.

Develop secondary characters

While secondary characters may not be the focus of the main action, their development can contribute significantly to the depth and complexity of the story as a whole.

One of the main functions of flashbacks and analepsis in secondary characters is to provide context and depth to their characterization. These techniques allow authors to explore secondary characters' pasts, revealing their experiences, desires, and hidden motivations. For example, a flashback might show a significant event in a secondary character's life that explains their present behavior or their relationship with the main characters.

Additionally, developing secondary characters through flashbacks and analepsis gives authors the opportunity to explore secondary themes and subplots that enrich the overall plot of the story. These characters can have their own unique challenges, desires, and story arcs that intertwine with those of the main characters, helping to create a richer, more nuanced narrative. For example, a flashback might reveal a secret or hidden connection between a secondary character and the main plot, adding suspense and tension to the story.

What's more, this technique can be used to create deeper emotional connections between characters and readers. When readers have a greater understanding of the backstories and motivations of secondary characters, they are more inclined to sympathize with them and emotionally invest in their story. This can lead to greater empathy and engagement from readers, thus enriching the overall reading experience.

In conclusion, the development of secondary characters through flashbacks and analepsis is a powerful narrative technique that allows authors to explore the story world and its characters in greater depth. Used with care and discernment, these tools can enrich the plot, characterization, and emotion of the story, giving readers a broader and more engaging perspective on the lives and relationships of secondary characters.

Integrate past and present

This integration requires a delicate balance between the two temporal dimensions, so that the past and present intertwine smoothly and coherently, contributing to the overall understanding of the story and characters.

One of the main challenges in integrating past and present is ensuring that flashbacks and analepsis are relevant and meaningful to the plot and character characterization. Each revelation about the past should have a clear narrative purpose and contribute to the overall theme of the story, whether by providing context, character development, or plot tease. For example, a flashback might reveal a hidden secret that changes the course of events in the present, creating suspense and tension in the narrative.

Furthermore, it is important that flashbacks and analepsis are integrated organically into the overall narrative structure of the story, avoiding abrupt interruptions or discontinuities that could distract the reader. Authors can use smooth transitions between past and present, using visual or linguistic cues to indicate temporal change and maintain clarity in the narrative. This ensures that readers can easily follow the story and understand the meaning of the information provided through flashbacks and analepsis.

Furthermore, the integration of past and present through flashbacks and analepsis can be used to create meaningful parallels and contrasts between the two temporal dimensions, highlighting changes and continuities in characters and plot over time. For example, a flashback might show a significant event in a character's youth, highlighting how their past experiences have influenced their behavior and choices in the present.

In conclusion, integrating past and present is a powerful narrative technique that allows authors to create a complex and nuanced narrative, enriching the story and offering readers a broader and more engaging perspective of the characters and events. Used with care and skill, these tools can improve the coherence and depth of storytelling, offering readers a richer and more fulfilling reading experience.

Create dynamic characters that evolve

A character with a well-defined narrative arc and emotional or psychological growth offers readers a richer and more satisfying reading experience, as they witness their development and transformation over the course of the story.

An **evolving character** is characterized by a significant change over the course of the story, which may concern their beliefs, their values, or their behavior. This change can be caused by key events, internal or external conflicts, or interactions with other characters. For example, a character might begin the story as a selfish, self-centered individual, but through the challenges and experiences he or she faces, learns the importance of compassion and selflessness, thus developing a story arc of redemption and personal growth.

A **dynamic character** is characterized by an emotional and psychological complexity that makes them realistic and three-dimensional. These characters have conflicting internal motivations, conflicting desires, and a natural evolution throughout the story. For example, a character might be tormented by internal doubts and uncertainties, struggling with the desire to do the right thing against his own weaknesses and fears. This complexity makes the character more interesting and engaging to readers, as they can identify with their challenges and internal conflicts.

To create dynamic, evolving characters, authors must carefully consider their backgrounds , motivations, and goals, as well as the conflicts that challenge them throughout the story. It is important that characters face significant challenges that challenge their beliefs and push them to grow and change throughout the story. Furthermore, it is essential that the characters react in a credible and authentic way to the circumstances that surround them, maintaining the coherence of their characterization and the verisimilitude of their evolution.

In conclusion, creating dynamic characters who evolve is an essential part of creative writing, as it significantly contributes to the complexity and depth of the narrative.

Exercise 21: Character analysis

Description: Choose a character from a book you love and analyze their characterization, background , motivations and narrative arcs. Write a short review that explores in detail the character's traits, key moments in his evolution, and his impact on the plot and other characters. Use this exercise to gain inspiration for developing your characters.

Exercise 22: Emotional depth

Description: Choose one of your main characters and write a series of internal monologues that explore their deepest and most complex emotions in different situations. Try to immerse yourself in the character's mind and explore their fears, hopes, desires and internal conflicts. This exercise is useful for making your character's characterization richer and more realistic.

Exercise 23: Comparison between characters

Description: Choose two main characters in your story and write a series of dialogues or scenes in which they interact with each other. Observe how they influence each other, how they react to each other's words and actions, and how their values, beliefs, and goals compare. Use this exercise to deepen the dynamics of the relationships between your characters and to reveal new facets of their personalities.

Chapter five

Practical Writing Exercises

"Creating perhaps means missing that step in the dance. It means giving that blow of the chisel into the stone."

ANTOINE DE SAINT-EXUPERY

Creative writing is an activity that requires constant exercise and practice to develop your skills and refine your style. This chapter offers a series of practical exercises designed to stimulate your creativity, deepen your character characterization, and develop the plot of your stories. By doing these exercises regularly, you can stimulate your creativity and generate new ideas that can enrich your stories and take your writing to new levels. Enough with the theory and happy writing!

Exercises to stimulate creativity

Exercises to stimulate creativity are essential to keep your imagination alive and to generate new ideas that can enrich your stories. Here are some practical exercises you can do to stimulate your creativity:

1. **Automatic writing** : Sit down with a pen and paper or in front of your computer and write freely for 10-15 minutes without interruption. Don't worry about grammar or coherence; let the words flow freely from

your mind. This exercise will help you overcome writer's block and unleash your creativity.

2. **Brainstorming** : Take a sheet of paper and write a word or phrase in the center. Then, draw lines branching out from that word, adding related or associated ideas. Continue expanding the diagram until you have generated a variety of ideas. This exercise will help you generate new ideas and explore different directions for your story.

3. **Free association exercises** : Take a word, image or phrase and associate it with words or concepts that come to mind. For example, if the word is "journey", you might associate it with words like "adventure", "exploration", "discovery", etc. This exercise will help you make unexpected connections and generate original ideas for your stories.

4. **Playing with words** : Pick a random word from a dictionary and try to use it in creative ways in a sentence or short story. Try exploring its literal and figurative meaning and finding new ways to express it. This exercise will help you expand your vocabulary and develop greater flexibility in your use of language.

5. **Telling visual stories** : Look at an image, photo, or illustration and create a story based on what you see. Ask yourself who the characters are, what their goal is, and what the main conflict of the story is. This exercise

will help you develop your ability to narrate visually and find inspiration in the images around you.

6. **Exploring "what if…"** : Take an ordinary situation or event and ask yourself what would happen if something extraordinary happened. For example, what would happen if an ordinary day suddenly turned into an extraordinary day? This exercise will help you think creatively and generate original ideas for your stories.

Writing prompt: starting from a sentence, an image, a situation

Writing from prompts, which can be a sentence, an image or a situation, is an effective method for starting the creative process and generating new ideas for writing. Here are some ways to develop this type of exercise:

1. **Suggestive sentence** : Start with a sentence that immediately captures the reader's attention and stimulates your imagination. It could be an intriguing phrase, a provocative question, or a cryptic statement. For example: "That day, in the silent forest, something unexpected happened", or "Close your eyes and imagine a world without borders".

2. **Evocative image** : Start with an image that inspires you and that can suggest a story or series of events. It could be a photo, a painting, or even a scene you imagined in your mind. For example, you might choose an image of

an old, rusty pocket watch, abandoned on an old wooden table, and imagine the story of whoever owned it and what they may have experienced.

3. **Intriguing Situation** : Imagine an unusual or extraordinary situation and think about how the characters might react to it. It could be a sudden storm during a picnic in the countryside, an unexpected encounter with a mysterious stranger, or a mysterious box found in the attic of an old house. These situations can be the starting point for a compelling and suspenseful story.

Once you've chosen your prompt, take some time to reflect on it and let your mind wander freely. Write whatever comes to mind, without worrying about the coherence or quality of the text. The goal is to unleash your creativity and generate new ideas that could become the basis for a larger story or complete narrative. Remember that there are no wrong answers in this type of exercise, so let your imagination guide you and enjoy the creative process!

Now let's go back to some exercises on topics already covered, with the difference that now you have all the tools to carry them out completely. It's time to connect all the dots.

Characterization exercises: describe a character from different points of view

Characterization exercises that involve describing a character from different points of view are extremely useful for developing a deep understanding of characters and making their characterization richer and more authentic. Here's how you can develop this type of exercise:

1. **Inside Point of View** : Begin by writing a short biography of the character, including details about his or her background , personality, goals, and fears. Then, write a short story or series of scenes from the character's perspective. Focus on his emotions, his thoughts, and his perceptions of the world around him. This will help you develop a deeper understanding of the character and create an authentic and believable voice for him.

2. **External Point of View** : Now change your perspective and describe the character from another character in the story. Choose a character who has a significant relationship with the main character and write a series of scenes or dialogue from his or her perspective. Consider how this character would perceive the main character, what impressions he would have of him, and how their relationship would influence his perception.

3. **Neutral observer's point of view** : Finally, try to describe the character from a neutral point of view, as if you

were observing from the outside. This could be done through third-person narration or through the point of view of an omniscient narrator. Focus on the character's physical traits, his visible behavior, and the general impressions he makes on other characters.

By doing these exercises, you will be able to explore your character from different angles and gain a more complete understanding of their personality and history. This will help you create more vivid, complex characters that resonate with readers and add depth and authenticity to your storytelling.

Plot development exercises: exploring different story lines and resolving conflicts

Plot development exercises are essential for creating compelling, well-structured stories. Exploring different story lines and resolving conflicts allows you to build a plot full of suspense and meaning. Here are some ways to develop this type of exercise:

1. **Exploring different narrative options** : Start with a basic idea for your plot and then try to explore different directions in which it could develop. Create a list of possible events, character choices, and turning points that could affect the course of the story. Explore alternative scenarios and consider how each could

change the fate of the characters and the final outcome of the story.

2. **Create internal and external conflicts** : Identify the main conflicts in your story and then think about how you might increase the tension and suspense by adding new conflicts or complications. These conflicts could be about the relationships between the characters, the external challenges they face, or their internal conflicts and personal struggles. Explore how these conflicts might interact with each other and how you might resolve them in a way that is satisfying to the reader.

3. **Resolve conflicts creatively** : Once you identify the conflicts in your story, think of creative ways to resolve them that are unexpected and meaningful. Avoid solutions that are too obvious or conventional and try to find an ending that surprises and satisfies the reader. It also considers the long-term consequences of the characters' choices and how these might affect their future and that of the story as a whole.

4. **Explore the consequences of your characters' actions** : Finally, reflect on your characters' actions and how they might affect the course of the story. Consider the decisions they make, their motivations, and the unintended consequences of their actions. Explore how character choices can impact the plot and other characters, and use these consequences to fuel tension and suspense in the story.

And now... a little madness!

Here we are, ready to immerse ourselves in a world of slightly "crazy" and creative exercises to stimulate your imagination and make your writing shine! Prepare to leave logic and rationality at the door as we venture into unusual and surprising literary territory. If you're ready to challenge convention and explore the roads less traveled in fiction, you're in the right place!

These exercises are like a playground for your mind, full of crazy challenges, endless possibilities and tons of fun. Get ready to reverse the rules, explore parallel worlds, and test the limits of your creativity. Sit back, buckle up and get ready for a wild and exciting journey through imagination!

Now, without further ado, grab your pen (or your keyboard) and let yourself be carried away by the wave of your crazy and absurd ideas that are about to come.

1. **Reverse roles** : Take two characters from your story and completely reverse their roles and defining characteristics. For example, if one is usually the protagonist, make them an antagonist and vice versa. Write a short scene or dialogue in which these new roles collide, exploring how it would change the dynamic between the characters and the course of the plot.

2. **The Character Test** : Choose one of your main characters and put him in an extreme or bizarre situation that forces him to act in unusual ways. For

example, present him with an impossible moral choice or make him face a series of absurd and unpredictable events. Write how the character would react to this situation and how this would affect his development and growth over the course of the story.

3. **Explore parallel worlds** : Imagine an alternate universe where the events of your story unfold completely differently. Rewrite a key scene or turning point in your plot, exploring how it would be different if circumstances were radically changed. Play with crazy and absurd ideas, letting your imagination roam freely through parallel worlds and infinite possibilities.

4. **The Random Word Game** : Take a book or dictionary and open it to a random page. Choose a word at random and use it as a starting point to write a short story or short story. The word doesn't need to make sense or fit the plot of your story; the goal is to challenge yourself to find a creative way to incorporate it into your writing and make it work in the story.

5. **Change genre** : Take your story and rewrite it in a completely different genre than the one in which it was conceived. For example, if your story is a thriller, turn it into a romantic comedy or epic fantasy. Explore how the characters, plot, and tone of the story would change based on your new chosen genre, letting your creativity express itself freely through new narrative and stylistic challenges.

6. **The literary crossover** : Choose two completely different literary worlds and imagine a crossover between them. For example, what would happen if Sherlock Holmes faced a mystery in the world of Harry Potter? Or what if Alice in Wonderland got lost in the Maze Runner maze? Explore how characters and settings would interact and adapt to new contexts, mixing the rules of different literary universes.

7. **Reverse dialogue** : Write a dialogue in which the characters communicate only through questions or only through answers, without ever using the other type of sentence. For example, one character might ask a series of questions and the other might respond only with affirmative or negative sentences. This exercise challenges you to find creative ways to advance the conversation and bring out the characters' personalities using just one mode of communication.

8. **The story backwards** : Write a story starting from the end and working backwards to the beginning. Start with the final moment of your story and work backwards to reveal how the characters got to that point. This exercise forces you to think nonlinearly and consider how past events have influenced the present, creating an intriguing and unconventional narrative.

9. **The story in shopping list form** : Write a story using only a list of seemingly random objects or actions, like a shopping list. For example, "Milk, eggs, bread... and an

alien invasion?" Each item on the list should inspire a new development in the plot, turning a seemingly random sequence of elements into a surprising and compelling story.

10. **The Nameless Character** : Write a story without ever revealing the protagonist's name. Use detailed descriptions and interactions with other characters to paint a vivid portrait of the protagonist without ever naming him directly. This exercise challenges you to find creative ways to bring out the character's personality and motivations without relying on their name.

Conclusions

By the end of this journey through the depths of creative writing, I hope you've found inspiration, knowledge, and practical tools to bring your stories to life. Writing is a never-ending art, a process of discovery and exploration that constantly challenges us to improve and grow. Whether you are an aspiring writer or a veteran navigating the waters of fiction, I hope this book has fueled your passion and commitment to the art of storytelling.

Always remember that every word you put on paper has the potential to transform into something magical, powerful and meaningful. Be bold in your approach, experiment, fail, learn and start again. There is no right or wrong path in creative writing, only your unique and personal journey towards creating something beautiful and authentic.

Continue to nurture your creativity, nurture your curiosity, and cultivate your unique voice in the world of fiction. Whether you're writing for yourself or for the world at large, your stories have value and importance. Face each page with courage and determination, knowing that your talent and passion can transform the world one word at a time.

With that, I wish you good luck in your writing journey. May you find joy, satisfaction, and success in your literary endeavors. And always remember, the world needs your stories. Never stop writing.